WHERE'S THE
LOVE
& WHO'S GOT MY
MONEY?

WHERE'S THE
LOVE
& WHO'S GOT MY
MONEY?

THE ANSWER TO HAVING IT ALL

JERI WALZ

DEDICATIONS

I would like to dedicate this book to my loving husband, Rod, and our amazing self-actualized adult children, Dan, Kym, Tyler and Wes.

Our children inspire us every day as they have honored themselves by going for their dreams.

Our son Dan discovered in college that he loved flying airplanes and so he made the decision to go for his dreams and become a commercial airline pilot. It was a long, hard road of dedication but he was clear of his vision and he held on to his dream and did whatever it took to achieve his goal. For years he was the bachelor pilot and proud of his reputation until one day he realized that what he really wanted was an honest, loving relationship with the woman of his dreams and to create a family together. It took some convincing but again he stayed true to his integrity and now he and his beautiful wife Korie are raising their children, Callie and Cooper, in a loving and supportive home.

Our daughter Kym is my heroine in life. She is the most amazing woman I know, who could have given into her challenges as a youngster and instead used them to propel her forward to a life of love and contribution. She runs a non-profit organization that is dedicated to supporting young people to be all that they can be. She facilitates seminars and is there for the kids in untold ways. She too created a family life for herself by marrying the man of her dreams, wonderful Kerry, who had already one son, Michael, and together, Kym and Kerry have two more amazing young sons, Zach and Jordan.

Our son Tyler, who we all thought would grow up to be a corporate attorney; has an insatiable appetite for information and devours and retains the most intricate details. He surprised us all when we discovered that his real passion in life was for musical theater. So he followed his dream and moved to Manhattan at age 25 where he performs on a regular basis. Tyler is producing an exciting play at this time, and is working on other fascinating projects including developing some interesting inventions he is bringing to market.

Tyler has in many ways been such a rock in our family, always seeing each of us for who we really are. He has an amazing ability to see right through us and supports us all being all that we can be. He remains single at this time but tells me marriage and children are in his future. He is gorgeous, ladies!

Our youngest son Wes grew up at a time when, for most years, I was able to leave the office to pick him up from school and take him to his many activities. My greatest joy was competing side by side with him in the hunter/jumper world for 10 years, starting when he was about 8 years old until he was 18. What a thrill it was to watch him ride.

He thrilled us too when he became passionate about personal growth work and immersed himself in it starting at age 19. He has gone on to become a fine young business entrepreneur in real estate investment, mortgage lending and recently co-founded a high-end auto-reconditioning company, Elite Finish Detailing. Wes, and his beautiful young bride Brandi, have just blessed us with a new granddaughter. She arrived in our arms on December 3, 2011. Her name is Journey Sofia Walz. We are so excited about Journey and so proud of Wes and Brandi. What an amazing team they are.

My husband Rod has been the greatest source of love and inspiration in my life. Together we have supported each other being all that we can be and loving each other for all that we are not. Together we built a successful business and raised our beautiful children. Rod has always taken care of the little girl who resides in me and reminds me of her when I forget. He has encouraged me in every endeavor. He was proud of me as I succeeded in business and applauded my advancement and growth. He was there for me as I followed my dreams competing in the horse world and he has been there for me when I decided to write this book. He has been there loving and supporting me each time I take on a new challenge, letting me know that he sees me as the capable woman that I am and never less. Without Rod, this book might still have been written but it would not have the same depth, as he was relentless in drawing me out as I wrote each chapter. Thank you, Rod. You are the love of my life and the man of my dreams.

ACKNOWLEDGMENTS

I would like to take just a moment to thank and acknowledge a few people who have helped me on this journey.

Without the assistance of my husband, Rod, and friend Liz Ragland, this book may never have been finished. Liz kept me on track and organized, while always inspiring me to keep going. Rod was relentless in having me dig deeper within myself to give more to you through this book. I am in gratitude to them both.

A special thank you to my nephew Geoff Hopf, a most gifted novelist and Bestselling author of "The End" and "The Long Road". These two books are the first of a series of books to come.

Geoff has always been a great student of life. He has the ability to see what is needed next to propel himself forward, while always making a difference in the lives of others. He is a loving and devoted husband to my precious niece Tahnee and an inspiring and fun loving Daddy to my grandnieces, Scarlette and Savannah.

Geoff, I thank you for inspiring me and supporting me in my journey as an author. I love you, AJ

To the many people who have wandered into my life at just the right time I am eternally grateful. There have been those special people who have contributed to this book as well. There are the many stories that people were willing to share and others who have read parts of my book as I was in the process of writing, and given me priceless feedback and encouragement. To Dr. Julie Van Putten, Teresa Keich, Dave Patton and Jan Gold. I give a heartfelt thank you. There are so many others, and you know who you are; I thank you. And, to all my students and clients I give a warm thank you for all your love and support.

I have had many teachers over the years but I would like to mention Dr. Chet Castellaw who was my first teacher of the principles of the Science of The Mind. I studied under him for ten years before he passed on to another realm.

I would like to thank my brother Jim who believed in me and helped to give me a great start in Real Estate and again as Rod and I started our company many years ago. He has always been a great example in my life of integrity and a standard to operate from in business. He is a devoted husband to my, amazing and beautiful sister-in-law, Jeanne, and father to my nephews Jonas and Damon and niece Tahnee W.

Thanks to my sister Jan, who even after her passing, many years later, continues to teach me to keep a sense of humor, in and about life.

My sister Judy has always seemed like the most fearless person I knew. As it turns out, I have finally learned that it wasn't that she was fearless; it is that she never lets her fear stop her from doing what she wants to do in life.

Judy's children, my nephew and niece, Neal and Tahnee, are like my own children. I love them as if they were my own.

Neal has been the man of that family since he was a little boy. He never stops taking himself on to be all that he can be. He is very successful young business man and a loving family man.

My niece Tahnee is my teacher. She exemplifies all that a woman can be. She has been a very successful business woman who now dedicates her life to her wonderful husband Geoff, who I love like a son, and their beautiful daughters, Scarlette and Savannah. She is beautiful, loving and giving. Tahnee is flirtatious with her husband and always lets him know that he is her man and the most important person in her life. She is amazing!

Last but not least, I want to thank my parents and my children. I am grateful to both my mother and my father for the lessons I have learned from each of them and for the love they bestowed upon me.

My children have all taught me so much and have given me more love than I could ever have imagined being possible. Thank you kids for your love and encouragement. I love you all.

These individuals have shaped my world and motivated me to reach for my full potential. They have taught me the true meaning of living my truth and inspired me to be all that I can be.

TABLE OF CONTENTS

Foreword   15

Prologue   21

1   What We Believe We Attract   27

2   What's Going on in That Mind of Yours?   47

3   Getting Out of Your Own Way   61

4   Your Life Beyond the Five Senses   73

5   New Understanding of the Laws We Never Break   85

6   Changing Your Patterns   103

7   Making Sense of the Oneness   125

8   Embracing the Unfamiliar   151

9   To Be or Not to Be   165

10 A Love Story about Money   187

A Conversation with the Author about Men and Women 209

Epilogue   219

FOREWORD BY LES BROWN

It has been said that in life you are either in the center of your strength, or in the center of your weakness. *Where's The Love & Who's Got My Money* is a guide to the center of your strength. This book takes you on a path that allows you to connect with and live from your authentic self. Each chapter is designed to provide you with a map to be in the driver's seat of your life, and to make things happen. It provides valuable tools for developing a larger vision of yourself beyond your mental conditioning, limited thinking, and your present circumstances. As your thinking changes, your beliefs about what is possible in your life will also change, and you will move into a richer, more abundant, fulfilling life.

Jeri's life is an example of the principles from which she writes with conviction and passion. Her life is a story of discovery regarding the things in life that really matter – joy, abundance, passion, love, self-fulfillment, and service. Despite periods of confusion, aloneness, loss, grief, and pain, she compels us to keep the faith, and to know that a life that you truly love is possible.

These key principles, based on Jeri's name, are evident as life principles throughout this book. They challenged me to continue to live my greatest life – the one that is yet before me. I offer them to you as you grow through each chapter in this book.

J – LIFE IS A JOURNEY.

Where's The Love & Who's Got My Money shows us that life is a journey to be explored, and to be experienced in all of its dimensions in order to find your true self. It is a winding road, which can sometimes feel like a roller coaster. But through it all, if you keep your head up, and your eyes straight ahead, you will develop a vision for an abundant life – a life that is only possible through your initiative.

E – EXPAND THE VISION OF YOURSELF.

Jeri's decision to expand her vision of what was possible for her life came from immersing herself in an inward journey to develop her authentic self. By doing this, she was able to connect with her personal power to achieve and accomplish goals beyond her wildest dreams. *Where's The Love & Who's Got My Money* is a lighthouse to lead us in the direction of our dreams. Regardless of where you are right now in your life, Jeri reminds you that you have greatness within you.

R – RELATIONSHIPS ARE REAL. THEY ARE A CURRENCY JUST LIKE MONEY.

Jeri's life is a visible demonstration that the greatest love you have is the one inside of you. She reinforces that all of us need to take the time to know who we really are. The closest relationships that we choose to develop and nourish reflect our inner consciousness and our vision for our lives. They show where you are going, not where you have been.

Jeri and her husband Rod's vision of their life together has resulted in a life of love, wealth, and contribution. They remind us to create within ourselves the type of qualities that we wish and desire in our closest friends, lovers, and life partners.

I – IMAGINE GREAT POSSIBILITIES FOR YOUR LIFE.

We are encouraged to live from our imagination rather than from our history. One of the key principles in this book is that you don't get in life what you want. You get in life what you are willing to imagine, believe, and develop. Einstein says, "The imagination is a preview of what's to come."

W – WORK IS ESSENTIAL FOR GROWTH.

Jeri believes that abundance is your birthright; however, working on yourself is the foundation for success. Nothing happens in life until you are you willing to do both the internal and external work to create a life of abundance.

A – ACCOUNTABILITY IS AS ESSENTIAL IN LOVE AS IT IS IN BUSINESS.

Jeri and Rod are both creators and supporters in a life that includes romance, love, and work. They are the glue that hold the worlds of love and money together, and create opulence and abundance not only in each other's life, but together as a supportive and encouraging team. They believe that a journey that is shared builds a richer and more expansive story. Jeri and Rod are believers in each other's growth, which is the foundation of their life journey.

L – LEGACY BUILDING SHOWS UP IN EVERY DIMENSION OF OUR LIVES.

Jeri challenges us to think in terms of service and contribution. Horace Mann says, "We should be ashamed to die until we have made some major contribution to human kind." Our children are 40% of our population, but 100% of our future. We see that legacy-building is about investing in our children and in the world around us. Kahil Gibran states so eloquently, "Our children will visit a world tomorrow that we will not see." Legacy-building is realizing that there is no success without successors, as evidenced by the incredible stamp that Jeri and Rod have made in the lives of their children. They have fostered in them the qualities of imagination and creativity, which have allowed them to find their purpose and passion in life.

Z – ZERO TOLERANCE FOR LIVING A LIFE OF MEDIOCRITY.

We live in a world where we are told more about our limitations than our potential. Jeri's life models a mindset of zero tolerance for being average. In order to make it today, you must be hungry to live a rich, meaningful, enjoyable life.

This book inspires you to create your greatest life. In this tough economy, the messages in *Where's The Love & Who's Got My Money* are a call to action to let go of our excuses for playing small, and to create a life that you can be proud of.

LES BROWN

About Les Brown...

If you have never heard Les Brown speak, you will want to; I promise you. He is a world-class speaker and teacher who has made a difference in the life of so many people. His personal story is powerful and inspiring and he has used the Universal Principles of life to turn his life from rags to riches and more importantly from someone who thought he could not make a difference in life to someone whose entire life is dedicated to just that. Have I mentioned that he inspires me every day?

In 2008, I was in training to be certified as a Life Coach when, for the first time, I heard Les Brown on a teleconference training call. Listening to Les that day, I was moved in a way that no one ever had moved me before. What I heard him say was that because he had found his voice, he is making a difference in many people's lives; that he had saved lives. He explained that each one of us has a special voice. I heard him loud and clear that only my voice can be heard by some. I intuitively knew when he said it that it was true. He said that we all have the responsibility to find our voice and share it with the world. We never know whose life we might save.

Les was also a presenter at the live training, in Florida, along with one of his daughters and other speakers he had been working with. Meeting him in person, I knew, in that moment, he was not like anyone I had ever met before. This is a man filled with love and compassion and a man who is loved by many. I have met many speakers and teachers in the personal development realm and no one has moved me like

Les Brown. This is why I asked him if he would be willing to write the forward to my book. Fortunately he was, and he did. What a gift.

Where's The Love & Who's Got My Money fits right in with the eloquent words of Les Brown when he challenged me to consider that it is my responsibility to not only find my voice, but more importantly to find my power voice, so that I can make a life-changing difference in the lives of many.

Les Brown's words, from his heart to mine, are always with me. I will continue to discover, develop and share my voice with those who are waiting for me. I encourage each of you to do the same. Your voice is unique and powerful. What have you been holding back? Whose life could you help to shape, or even save, if only you were willing to find your voice and share it with the world?

With love,

PROLOGUE

When I set out writing this book, I struggled for a title that would describe what's inside and hopefully evoke a reaction so someone would read it. When I initially bounced the title off some friends, they acted surprised because the title, as a question, almost sounds like a victim statement. However, my intention is actually to reach the brave, authentic you inside who is willing to explore and challenge the old inherited beliefs you hold about yourself and enrich your ability to create love and money in your life.

I have experienced my struggle and have seen many friends' struggle with creating love and money in our lives. Some people think that love and money are unrelated; however, I have seen and experienced firsthand how the two intertwine. This book was written from love and definitely with a specific expectation of financial gain; that specific expectation has nothing to do with me, but rather with you. I have been blessed in my life by my love and money journey and nothing means more to me than to have you receive something life-changing out of this book.

When you consider that money flows like oxygen it cannot help but intertwine with love. Those who struggle financially understand how one can affect the other. If the love isn't flowing, the money seems to slow down and if the money slows down the feeling of love can be diminished because of distraction and worry. The opposite is also true, that if the love is flowing, money finds a way to it and if the money flows then love is not distracted and can flourish. This obviously is not true for everyone and many people are enriched by living a simpler life without money as a focus. This is their blessing. I wrote this book for every one of you to choose for yourself what lessons are important for your growth, regardless of whether it is in the area of love or money or both. My life's journey is full of examples that are easily recognizable by all. It's time for you to make a stand and change the flow of your thoughts once and for all.

WE DON'T ALWAYS GET WHAT WE WANT BUT WE DO GET WHAT WE BELIEVE IN.

The principles in this book are awaiting you to embrace them. When you read about them it may seem so obvious that you should embrace them, yet the enemy within, that old voice that loves to keep you in familiar thought, speaks to you incessantly, and for many, will win almost every time. For that reason alone, <u>it is critical to feel the pain of knowing that nothing will change on its own</u>. You must break through and create new thought to have what you say you want in your life. We don't always get what we want but we do get what we believe in. We co-create the results in our life with our thoughts. The results that you currently have in the area of love and money were set in your mind years ago. For some, this is a big yikes!!!!

I am going to share with you examples from my life and others so that you may vicariously experience how the Universal Laws and life forces are at work, 100% of the time. Use these examples well as tools to open up discoveries and epiphanies within yourself. It is my deepest desire for you to experience the fullness of life that is available to us all, if you choose it. It is also truly my wish that you will have multiple breakthroughs throughout the reading of this book that will change the course of the rest of your life's journey. For some, it may be a small change, much like the trim tab on a sailing ship that makes miniscule adjustments to maintain a successful course, and for others it may be highly significant and life-changing. Either way, enjoy the journey.

LANGUAGE

One of the things I have discovered in working with people is there is often a language barrier, even when we speak the same native tongue. In this book, I will be discussing with you my beliefs, my experiences and things that I have discovered about love and money so it is important that we be on the same "languaging" page so that you can gain value from the principles I discuss. One topic, for example, will be about spirit and our connection to others. Some of my readers and clients are religious or at least come from a religious background and understand that what I am saying is in harmony with religious thought. Others may consider themselves agnostic, meaning that they do not believe in a higher power or connection yet are still open to considering there could be more to our existence. However, if you are committed to the idea that there is no higher force at play and no connection, then I suggest you put the book back on the shelf, for this particular book will not resonate with you in any way.

I have studied Metaphysics for over forty years and have read many books and listened to many spiritual teachers over the years. I have worked with many different people of different walks of life with different backgrounds. Often I discover that if I listen very carefully to what the other person is saying, they may use different "languaging" than I, but when I listen carefully through the words chosen, we usually mean very close to the same thing. We often get to the same result in our soul, our heart and our manifestation; however, the way we explain the phenomena that transpires sounds often very different.

I am going to be discussing with you a higher power throughout this book. I often refer to the higher power as "The One Life Force", "The Universe", "Infinite Intelligence" or "Infinite Power and Love". I may refer to this higher power as "God". You may have other names that you call this higher power; the power does not care what you call it.

The truth is this higher power is an inexplicable force that is in our lives at all times. We can either tap into it consciously or not, but it exists whether or not we acknowledge it. Now this is a definitive statement that those disbelievers would say I cannot know this to be true. As I stated in the beginning, this is my expression of what I have discovered to be true in life. I am completely open to new ideas. As I evolve I continue to discover more each day; and what I seem to discover is, without question, there is a Life Force that is greater than we are as individuals and we are all its expression.

So, I will do my best to share with you what I have discovered to create a successful life filled with love, joy, health, prosperity and romance. I hope that there are some pearls within these chapters for you. What I know is, if you are open to receive them, they will be there for you. So take a look inside and see how open you are right now, or notice if your mind is already closing down and being judgmental about what you have read so far.

I know that you already know instinctively that you can be more, do more and contribute more. You know that there is more of you than you have been willing to express, or felt capable of expressing so far in your life. Maybe you are willing but are not sure how. If you are ready to stretch yourself into more of who you are meant to be, enjoy your journey as you read on. I am going to share with you my own story and the stories of others throughout the book and give you some practical things you can do to expand yourself into the great life you were meant to live.

Enjoy!

CHAPTER 1
— WHAT WE BELIEVE WE ATTRACT —

Will you live the cosmic adventure?
Look for the good wherever it is and add to
it.

–Dr Harry Morgan Moses

1
CHAPTER

I grew up in San Diego, CA, and as a little girl I was so in love with my Daddy. He was my hero and symbolized all the good in the world. In my eyes, the sun rose and set in him. Passionate about life, he worked and played hard and loved flying his plane. I loved being with him in his plane, as I knew how much he loved it. He was an excellent pilot. Both his physical stature and his presence filled a doorway and it seemed to me that all who knew him loved and admired him. One day, when I was in the third grade, my mother and father decided not to be married anymore. That was such a blow to me. How could they just decide not to be my parents? I was born to them; they were my parents; I didn't understand how this could be a decision. At first, Daddy left our home and my sisters and brother and I stayed with our mother for a time. Then my sister Judy and I went to live with Daddy.

GIFTS COME TO US OFTEN IN DISGUISE.

When I was going into the fourth grade, Daddy decided it was in my sister's and my best interest to go away to boarding school in Ojai, CA, while he launched a new business that required much of his time and travel. I remember how terrified I was when he flew us up and took us to that school. Certain that the teachers and students would torture and kill me, I couldn't understand how my Daddy could leave me there to this torturous fate that was so real in my mind. Of course, none of this occurred and in many ways the lessons I learned there carried me through life with a strength I may not have known otherwise. **Gifts come to us often in disguise.**

During my first few months at boarding school, I was afraid and often felt very alone with no parents near to tuck me in at night, so even though I had not been raised with any religion, I reached out and started to pray every night. Little

EMBRACE YOUR CURRENT SITUATION.

by little, certain truths began to reveal themselves and what I discovered is that God lives inside me and all around me. I discovered that I was never alone and that I was connected to something bigger. I started writing poetry and was amazed by the incredible words that flowed through me as though spoken by someone who was using me to express them. Through this vehicle, love poured from me and into me simultaneously and I began to give myself permission to dream of the life that I wanted someday. I allowed my mind to create very clear and specific pictures. I dreamed of having horses and I dreamed of a husband by my side who would love and cherish me. I dreamed of a family and home filled with love. I dreamed and I dreamed and these dreams gave me life.

I gave myself permission to see that the life I had been dreaming of would become my reality, and with this knowing, I was able to get through difficult times. I now knew someday I would have a life of my own creation. Because I believed my future was set, I was able to finally let go of the fears and sorrow and embrace my current situation. I became open to the gifts in my situation. I learned to ride horses and made friends who soon became more like family. Since we all shared the common experience of being away from our parents and homes, we made the school our home and each other our siblings; this worked well.

After three years of boarding school, my Daddy felt he could limit his travel and so he brought us home to Mission Valley in San Diego, CA. At the time, this area was still fairly rural and Daddy bought me my first horse as well as one for himself. Our next door neighbors had kids my age and they too had horses and loved to ride. Every day my next door neighbor and I jumped on our horses bareback and spent the entire day racing around Mission Valley. That summer was the best summer of my life.

Daddy had also purchased a ranch for us with twenty-six acres, stables and our own landing strip for our plane. This was an amazing dream come true. We were scheduled to move in, in a couple of months. As life sometimes does show up differently than we planned, it did this time too. Two days before school was to start, on his return flight home from a business trip, Daddy's plane went down in a storm over Texas. My Daddy, the love of my life, was gone forever. At that time it seemed that all my dreams were gone with him. I was twelve years old at the time. My poor mother could not console me and I withdrew from everyone. I felt this was my loss alone and was so caught up in my own grief that I was unaware that anyone else could be suffering from what seemed to be my own personal tragedy. This seemed the final blow for me. All I wanted now was to be dead and be with my Daddy. All that kept me from taking my own life was the thought that my Daddy would not be proud of me for this action, and wouldn't want me with him that way.

Life seemed so difficult. Every day was just one more day I had to endure until my own death. At twelve years old and even through high school, I wished for death to come soon for me. I remember sitting on the roof of the Mission Valley house and remembering that Daddy told me one day he would take me to ends of the earth. Angry with him for not keeping his word, I made a decision that altered the course of the rest of my life; that if my Daddy could leave me so could everyone else. I realized that the only one person on this earth that would never leave me was me. This realization worked for and against me in life. While it made me strong and independent, it also kept me from fostering lasting intimate relationships.

NOTICE WHAT YOU ARE ATTRACTING AND SEE IF IT IS FAMILIAR TO FEELINGS YOU HAD AS A CHILD.

I created a pattern of attracting relationships that were doomed to failure. When a relationship ended, my initial tears over the person who left inevitably led to hysterical wailing, "Daddy, Daddy, why did you leave me?" It wasn't until I was 30 years old before I realized that I was the one sabotaging the relationship in order to recreate the tragedy of my father's death over and over again. I know that sounds crazy but that is exactly what I would do. Whether we are aware of it or not, we all tend to attract what is familiar to us. For me it was pain and loss, especially that of my Daddy. Notice what you are attracting and see if it is familiar to feelings you had as a child. They may not be the feelings you now desire but they are familiar and you are drawn to them even if you don't like them. Not to fear, we will be covering this more in later chapters and more importantly, how to turn this around to create what you do want.

So, for the first time, at 30 years old, I chose life. I realized finally that Daddy lived his life and part of that experience was crashing his plane. What I can say for him is he always lived his life to the fullest and went out doing what he loved. I choose the same for me now.

ATTRACTIVE FORCES

It is important to give yourself permission to search inside yourself for your vision of who you can be; what is Life's plan or God's plan for you? As I shared with you earlier, I reached a point in my life where I didn't even want to live. Even after many years of studying and applying the principles that you'll learn in this book, I still, at times, forget who I am and find myself thinking that I haven't accomplished enough in my life. How insidious that personal hammer can be. In reality we are all in a constant state of remembering and forgetting who we are. For me, this occurs daily as I go about my life; I often get caught up in my daily activities and am unconscious of my greatness. It's a choice to stop and remind ourselves who we are. In truth, we are all perfect, whole and complete; in other words, **we are a perfect idea**

> WE EXPRESS LIFE AT THE LEVEL OF OUR AWARENESS.

created, and we express life at the level of our awareness.
Just as my dreams were the seeds upon which my life
unfolded when I was a frightened little girl in boarding
school, you, whatever your age, can create a picture of what
you want. By giving yourself permission to have it, you will
attract it to you. That is the simple version, however, in
reality there are forces energetically that are in play, and your
state of mind and heart affect this energy and your results.

The Law of Attraction (like attracts like) has been in
play in my life and of course in your life also. I just didn't
realize what it was and neither do most of us. It is always
working. When you understand that we are connected and
that the Law of Attraction is at play at all times, this allows
us to intentionally manifest the results
in our lives. While my life as a young
girl was one of depression and thoughts
of suicide, what I did not realize is the
depressive thoughts and feelings that
I held were "attracting" to me exactly
what I got. As a result, life seemed hard
and sad.

> SEARCH INSIDE
> YOURSELF FOR
> YOUR VISION OF
> WHO YOU CAN BE.

What you think, you become. So often we blame others
for our unhappiness and undoing. In my case, ultimately
I realized that I was the one causing my own unhappiness
and I was the one getting in my own way in regards to
relationship and financial success. This realization is the first
step to freedom. Tired of running into brick walls, I turned
my life around by changing the way I thought about myself
and others. What happened is that as I began to change the
way I was looking at the events and circumstances in my life,

my life began to change for the better. I literally began to "attract" to me a new way of life.

You see, like me, and everyone else on the planet, you are always either in creation mode or in the effect of your circumstances, thoughts and beliefs. Some time ago, a dear friend of mine, Shayne, who is more like a daughter to me, and is also my horse trainer, came to me as she struggled with a decision regarding the direction she would take her business. She was always clear from childhood that she would be a horse trainer and teach others to ride and compete in the hunter/jumper show world, but she reached a point in her career where she was confused about whether she should spend more time working the A show circuit or stay in the county level show circuit. She was most definitely the queen trainer in her world but she wanted to keep pushing herself to be more; to be the best trainer she could be. Committing to the A show circuit would mean a lot more travel time and a different clientele. As we discussed this together and after much introspection, she finally realized that she was happy with the clientele that she had created and attracted to her. She loved going to county level shows where it seemed that the families were involved on a loving level. They supported their children and all the other competitors. The A circuit was more just down to business and the competition didn't seem as friendly.

IT'S A CHOICE TO STOP AND REMIND OURSELVES WHO WE ARE.

What she ultimately realized was that she could continue to grow as a professional and continue to be the best trainer she could be and compete at the shows that were fun and fulfilling to her. She is still the queen of the county circuit and yet she has grown her A show circuit business organically. She started importing top quality horses for her clients and developing them to compete at any level. They all enjoy the local shows and also travel to particularly fun and prestigious shows where her clients compete and win against the top horses and riders in the country. Her business is booming and now she is working on finding balance with family and career. So life goes on.

We attract to ourselves the challenges we are ready to deal with at any point in time. Shayne was at a crossroads, she felt. She thought she was not showing up with all that she had for herself. Her clients were doing well but she knew there was more of her to give. She wanted to expand her skills and professionalism; I would venture to say her reputation in the horse community. There were other trainers that she admired and aspired to emulate. She thought she would have to give up what she loved in order to be an A show circuit trainer. In the end, she didn't have to give up anything. She made some minor changes to how she does business and she brought her clients along with her. She and her clients at Chestnut Hills Equestrian Center are something to be reckoned with at any horse show.

EXPRESS WITHIN YOURSELF THE QUALITIES YOU WANT TO ATTRACT IN SOMEONE ELSE.

As I learned to shift my thoughts to creation, my business grew steadily and I created the ranch that I always wanted. I then set out to "attract" the love of my life by becoming very clear of the qualities I wanted in my life partner. I wrote down the qualities that I was seeking and then set out to embrace, within myself, those very qualities. By doing so, I was laying the groundwork for the relationship of my dreams. Not surprisingly, at 30 years of age, I attracted the perfect life-partner in Rod. For example, if you want a life-partner who is kind and compassionate, those are qualities you need to discover and express within yourself. If you desire someone who is considerate and patient, guess what, you need to discover and express those qualities as well. I cannot express enough how important it is to embrace what I just shared.

The naïve belief is to expect someone else to have those qualities and, in essence, help save you from yourself. The Law of Attraction requires that you find and grow those qualities within yourself if you expect to attract someone with them. Think of it this way; if such a person did exist, the honest question to answer is, why would they want to be with you if you did not have those qualities also?

What are the qualities you seek in a life partner and mate? As you think of these things, I suggest you write them down and be as specific as possible yet avoid things that are situationally oriented; such as: he or she drives a particular kind of car or has a particular kind of job or business or has had certain experiences in life. Think of qualities that are of the "human spirit". For me, the quality that I loved the most about Rod was his passion for personal growth. I had that passion also so it is no mystery as to why we connected. What's wonderful is that this still remains a passion that we share today, even more.

Rod and I chose marriage 10 months after we started dating. We are now married over 30 years, and it just gets better every year. We have a vibrant, active relationship that includes four amazing and self-actualized children, as well as a highly successful business. It was, and is, based upon the principle that we attract to ourselves exactly what we think and believe in addition to contributing value to the lives of all who are involved at any level; from our clients, to our employees and the stockholders as well. It is a true win-win. As a result, our company has been highly ranked, multiple years, as one of the fastest growing companies in the U.S. by INC 500 Magazine.

WHEN YOU UNDERSTAND THAT WE ARE CONNECTED AND THAT THE LAW OF ATTRACTION IS AT PLAY AT ALL TIMES, THIS ALLOWS US TO INTENTIONALLY MANIFEST THE RESULTS IN OUR LIVES.

I know that you are interested in creating a romantic, wonderful relationship and you want more money in your life or you probably wouldn't have picked up this book. You may be wondering; "Where is the love in my life?" and "Who's got my money?" Look inside yourself and be honest about what really makes you happy and fulfilled. Don't try to be something that you think someone else would want you to be or that you think would make you look better. Always follow your heart, your passion. If you do this and give it all you've got, you can have it all.

WHAT DID LIFE POUR INTO YOU?

If you've ever planted a garden, you first have to look at the condition of the soil. The success of your garden depends a lot on the quality of the soil. The same is true with our beliefs. Each of us has grown in a soil of beliefs that was <u>created by others</u> in the formative years of our life. What I mean by that is when you were born you had no filter and took in, without question, all the input from others, especially those closest to you. Out of this you formed a set of beliefs, a personality, which endures today. This is not good or bad. It is simply the way you are made up. The good news is that we have dominion over our thoughts and we are not stuck with what got poured in. In order to fully experience what I'm about to discuss here, it may be good to think for a moment about the fundamental beliefs that were poured into you.

EACH OF US HAS GROWN IN A SOIL THAT WAS CREATED BY OTHERS IN OUR LIFE AT THAT TIME WHEN WE WERE A CHILD.

A great way to understand this is to ask yourself the question; when did you choose to speak English (or whatever your first language is)? This may seem like an odd question, because the truth is you didn't choose your language. It was poured into you like so many other ideas and beliefs about relationships and money. Most research shows that by the age of four, 50 percent of your personality and beliefs about your ability to be loved and to love are already in place. As you continue to age from four to eight and beyond, roughly another 35 percent of your beliefs are formed, including absorption of your parents and other influential people's beliefs about money and relationships based upon their situation at that time. My daughter Kym (from Rod's first marriage) is a good illustration of how the beliefs poured into us affect our life.

THIS IS KYM'S STORY IN HER OWN WORDS.

"I grew up in the Hamptons. Not necessarily the Hamptons as you might envision it with all the glamour and glitz. Mine was a little different, as my childhood included public assistance, a single-parent home at a time when there were very few, and an experience void of happiness and love. I would often drive by the big houses, with the big lawns, and wonder what that experience was like and wonder why I was not that 'lucky'. I often referred to them as the 'shiny people'; almost resenting 'them' at times.

The women in my life, my primary role models, were women who were hardened by their past experiences. Women who chose men that were riddled with addiction, physically abusive, or emotionally unavailable. They were heavy in the heart and carried much anger. At the same time they were women that did the best they could and ensured my most basic needs were met.

I was in my pre-teens when I first met Jeri (Mom). She was married to my dad. My relationship with my dad was new at the time, and they lived on the other coast. My first communication with her was in a letter both she and Dad had written. His letter was a condensed version of hers. Hers was pretty; her handwriting had those extra touches that added that something special. The letter brought me up-to-date on the happenings of their lives, their marriage, the birth of my baby brother and the hope of a newfound relationship with them. I remember so wanting to meet her, yet feeling the need to be loyal to my biological mom.

Soon after receiving that letter they traveled to New York. They came to my house to pick me up to visit with them. This was the first time I had seen her. She was beautiful. She had makeup on and nice clothes and smiled when she talked. Her voice was light and comforting. Even at this young age I couldn't believe my dad had been married to both of these women in one lifetime. Jeri was certainly one of the 'shiny people'. I traveled with them to Massapequa, at times in total conflict. I began to like her and yet somehow felt as if I was betraying all the other women in my life, and everything I had believed.

Later that evening Jeri received a call telling her that her horse needed to be put to sleep. She was devastated and I felt helpless. I felt myself starting to melt. I was experiencing what I know now to be compassion, and yet again I was in conflict. I wanted to stay angry at my dad and her for past hurts, I wanted to make it difficult on my dad, I wanted them to know how angry I was, and how much they messed up, and yet there I was melting, with my heart breaking right alongside of her for a creature I had never met.

I believe the horse's name was 'Lady', which interestingly enough is so symbolic to me. You see, as a survivor of sexual abuse I held these beliefs of who I was as a woman. I certainly did not see myself as a 'young lady'. I had this silly notion that being a lady meant I was weak. I purposely never wore pink. I thought I needed to be tough, angry, and, yes, tomboyish to be considered 'real'. Jeri was a lady and yet she was strong, powerful and driven. Here I was, 14 years old, and my step-mom and my dad were shiny people . . . and yet I kind of liked them. This was going against much of what I thought to be true at the time. Much of what I had learned.

I began visiting California regularly. I am certain my relationship with my dad is what it is today as a result of her hard work. She was the heart of all of it. I would visit in the summers and we grew our relationship over the phone. I would sit in the backseat and watch her gently scratch the back of my dad's neck as she sang along to the radio. She certainly did not need the radio; her voice alone was majestic. As silly as it sounds, that experience was new to me, two people showing affection, loving each other as they drove down the road. I was being shown love.

This would be a constant lesson over the years, the lesson of love. She showed it in every action. She loved her animals to her core, she loved my brothers, she loved my dad, and she loved me, even in the moments I felt unlovable. She brought love to everything. It was behind every word, every action, and every moment.

WE ARE OFTEN JUST REPEATING WHAT WE LEARNED AS A CHILD EARLY ON WHEN WE WERE PRIVY, BOTH CONSCIOUSLY AND UNCONSCIOUSLY, TO OUR PARENT'S BELIEFS AND PREJUDICES REGARDING MONEY AND PEOPLE WITH MONEY.

Especially when she was challenging me to be better, do better, and go higher. Jeri would gently remind me when I was feeling disconnected, that I was equally a part of this family. As blended as we were, our uniqueness is what our strength was. She kept on loving me unconditionally with no conditions! She showed me how to be a mom, how to value who I was, and how to love. She loved me as a girl through to my own motherhood and called me to a higher level of self. When I need a kick in the ass, a spiritual tune-up, if you will, it is Jeri that I call. She may use words like "darling" and "cute", two of which do not roll off my tongue so easily, but she is one tough momma, and has a strength and conviction I sit in awe of. She has helped me find my light and as a result I can begin to see myself as one of the "shiny" ones."

–Kym Walz Laube

Kym is my hero. She was able to discover her truth regardless of what was poured into her. She has overcome so much in her life and is now surrounded by love that she has created. Kym is one the most loving and giving people

I know. She used the lessons in her life, as painful as many were, to grow and create the life of her dreams. She could have chosen another path and no one would have blamed her. Her choice was for life and love. She gives and receives love and that is a daily choice we can all make.

Each of us has the choice each day to choose to be a victim of our circumstances or to choose our own path. Your story is unique to you; however, the principles work the same for each of us. No matter what you may have faced in your life, you have the choice right now to "rewrite" your story. You can choose to discover the gifts that are there for you or you can tell the same story over and over as though you have no choice in how your life is created. I am here to tell you that you can create your life anew. It takes courage sometimes to face ourselves squarely but it is the only way to be free.

What preconceived ideas do you hold about love based on your early experiences? Let's talk about the love in your life right now.

Have you ever found yourself observing a couple who seems so interested in each other and you can sense the love between them and you wish you had a relationship like that? Did you hear an internal voice telling you that you couldn't have that? Where does that voice come from and what is its purpose? You see that others seem to be in relationships that are working. Why is it that your relationships do not feel satisfying? Maybe you are not in a relationship or maybe you're in one now, yet you still feel alone. If you are honest with yourself, you know that relationships can work, because there are a lot of couples out there who seem to be okay; in fact, some seem downright happy, don't they?

If you really want a relationship, see it clearly in your mind as you wish it to be, even if you are redefining an existing one. See all the qualities of the person you wish to attract to you and then become that person. Begin to embrace those qualities within yourself. If you have an internal voice telling you that you are incapable of creating a wonderful relationship then politely or not-so-politely tell that voice to "shut up". This is not up for debate; we attract to ourselves where we are coming from in our belief systems. We attract likeminded people to ourselves; this is why it is so important to become the qualities you wish to attract. If you want to know what you have believed about relationships, look around you and see what you have created so far. If this is not the picture you want then we have some work to do but the good news is you can create whatever you want; however, the price of admission is that you must be willing to grow.

Now let's touch on money in your life. Have you ever asked yourself *what you _believe_ about money*? Most of us typically would not ask this of ourselves. Yet, this burning question is the foundational soil through which you express your level of desire and willingness for financial success. We will go into more detail later, but suffice it to say that what you believe about money is the foundational soil for your ability to attract it into your life. If you wonder if you actually have a belief about money, then complete the following catch phrases: "Money is the root of all _____" or "Money doesn't grow on _____". If your answers were automatic, you can be assured that they are an indicator of foundational beliefs you have about money.

Typically, we learned these phrases from someone close to us, often a parent, who wanted to instill their own thoughts about money. Like a fish that doesn't see the water, we don't see the inherited thoughts and internal beliefs that drive what we attract to ourselves regarding money. We are often just repeating what we learned as a child early on when we were privy, both consciously and unconsciously, to our parents' beliefs and prejudices regarding money and people with money. Take a look at your beliefs about money; are they creating the lifestyle you desire for you and your family?

In today's world where we have all experienced, at some level, the economic collapse created by greed and false appreciation such as in real estate, now more than ever, it is important to discover your internal and learned beliefs about money and your relationship with it in order to create and attract more money into your life. Begin by examining what you believe about money. Determine who you would be if you had the money you wanted in your life and explore your willingness to let go of past beliefs and embrace the concept that your thoughts about money and your relationship with it will determine how much flows your way.

Have you noticed that even today, in this difficult economic climate, there are people who find a way to grow financially? So you know it can be done. *By the way, money doesn't care who has it, so why not you?* Remember, in order to create what you want, you must focus on what you want rather than on what you don't want. For example, if you focus on being "out of debt", then you are focusing on the debt. That is what you don't want. Even if you say that you *want* to make a lot of money, you are still focusing on the *wanting.* Once again, that is what you don't want. To focus on what you want, you must think of abundance. See it in your mind; money flowing in and your bank balances abundant. When you get to the feeling of assuredness that it is handled, you will begin to see the results. You have to believe in the abundance in your life. When you can really own it and know it in your soul, you start to see the manifestation in your reality.

Something to ponder: the highest amount of money that you have ever earned in a year is a key indicator of your money-consciousness. We often look for the next job or next opportunity to bust through, yet, rarely do we look within for the answers. Foundational beliefs, poured into you as a child, shape and control the financial results in your life. By becoming keenly aware of those beliefs that were imprinted on your mind early on, you can begin the process of addressing the changes in your thinking that will facilitate and attract expanded financial results. If you are still left wondering, be patient, as we will touch on the topics of Love and Money in more detail later. We need to do some work here so we'll spend some time exploring some of the more obvious, yet misunderstood, fundamentals about how we learn and how we operate.

CHAPTER 2

— WHAT'S GOING ON IN THAT MIND OF YOURS? —

*If you are carrying strong feelings
about something that happened in
your past, they may hinder your
ability to live in the present.*

–Les Brown

2
CHAPTER

Our thoughts have the answer to *Where's The Love & Who's Got My Money?* The problem is that many of us don't know where to look for those answers. The secret lies in knowing what's going on in that mind of yours. Many of your thoughts were passed down to you from your parents and other influential people in your life; people like teachers, coaches, ministers and others. So then why do the thoughts of our earliest influences become our own?

THE SECRET LIES IN KNOWING WHAT'S GOING ON IN THAT MIND OF YOURS.

As a child, your mind isn't fully developed and is similar to a sponge in that it absorbs every word in which it comes into contact, without any filter. In the early stages of development, you were influenced by all of your experiences and took in the attitudes and beliefs of those with whom you were closest. For those of you who were blessed with vital, growing parents this input was uplifting and set the stage for your success later on. However, for those of you who were not so blessed, you may have been taught that you may be less than worthy of your own success and happiness. In most cases, our parents meant well and were just trying to protect us from disappointment. Remember that as a child we do not vote on the value of what gets poured in; we just absorb it and construe the words of others about us as truth and, in some cases, this can be damaging to our self-esteem and confidence.

If you want to rewire your thought process, you first need to understand that for much of your daily life you are on automatic pilot and your mind is the driving force. It takes a willing and conscious effort to consider changing your mind and have the courage to examine your old beliefs. The reward is that once you do, you choose your thoughts rather than being at the mercy of them. To do this, we need to examine the makeup of the mind. Your mind is separated into three states of consciousness: the conscious, the subconscious, and the Super-Conscious or Super Infinite Intelligence. This doesn't mean to infer that you have three minds, but that these various states are coexistent. Each of these is so important that I'm going to discuss them individually.

> IT TAKES A WILLING AND CONSCIOUS EFFORT TO CONSIDER CHANGING YOUR MIND AND HAVE THE COURAGE TO EXAMINE YOUR OLD BELIEFS.

THE CONSCIOUS MIND

The conscious part of the mind uses the five senses: sound, taste, touch, smell, and sight. It functions by using logic and free will to accept or reject any idea. As I mentioned earlier, you were influenced by your earliest mentors and because these beliefs were given to you by people who loved you and/or cared for you at such an early age, it is hard for you to question them. Some people live their entire lives basing their actions and behavior on these early thoughts. You don't have to live in this manner. Why? Because you have dominion over your own thoughts. No person or circumstance can make you choose what you think about.

You must learn to be very selective about the thoughts that you hold in your conscious mind. You must become aware of and filter the thoughts that you are bombarded with everyday; at work, watching TV, listening to the radio or even the conversations that you either participate in or are around you that you do not consciously filter. Now, let's move on to the subconscious mind.

> TO REWIRE YOUR THOUGHT PROCESS, YOU FIRST NEED TO UNDERSTAND THAT FOR MUCH OF YOUR DAILY LIFE YOU ARE ON AUTOMATIC PILOT AND YOUR MIND IS THE DRIVING FORCE.

THE SUBCONSCIOUS MIND

The subconscious mind is the sum total of our past experiences and memories. What we feel, think, or do forms the basis of our experience. At this state of consciousness, our habits and beliefs are formed. This is where all of your memories are stored including those early impressions from parents and others in our early childhood when the Conscious Mind was not developed yet. Since the subconscious mind has no ability to reject any idea or thought, it simply accepts every suggestion made to it. Let me point out, however, it is the repetitive thoughts that become ingrained beliefs. So as mentioned above, as a child, all thoughts and ideas were poured into the subconscious unfiltered.

Your self-image, for example, consists of memories which have an emotional connection to the past; these memories cannot help you when attempting to break negative thought patterns. It is important to rewrite the story from a different perspective so that your memories create a positive effect.

Your subconscious mind has no choice but to accept what you think. It has to accept the pictures you give it. Every thought you choose to let into your subconscious mind is recorded and stored. One of the fundamental principles in Metaphysics is, "whatever the mind can conceive and believe it can achieve." As I studied, I was told that I could create in my life whatever I believed. When I heard this, I knew I was screwed because I didn't for a moment believe, back then, that I could be financially successful or create the incredible relationship that I now have with Rod.

Your subconscious mind always gives you back what you believe. I used to have a belief that I always got the flu over Christmas. Year after year, I succumbed to this belief every holiday season. Once I realized that this was my belief system and I had dominion over my thoughts, I gave up that belief and I haven't been sick during the holidays since. We're not stuck with those thoughts, so once you realize this, you can change your life.

It is important that we till our soil and become aware of our beliefs. A key to success is nothing more than becoming aware of your thoughts and consciously choosing them. The truth is we are all spiritual beings connected to the Infinite Intelligence. Know that in this book, you'll learn how to become more consciously aware of your potential by understanding the mind and how it works and the realization of your connection to the Infinite Intelligence. As you read through the remaining pages, you'll learn how to course-correct those thoughts that do not support you in your quest for a healthy, happy, prosperous life.

INVITE YOUR MIND TO SEND UP HAPPY, PEACEFUL, AND FULFILLING THOUGHTS THAT WILL EMPOWER YOUR LIFE.

Whatever repetitive thoughts you hold will determine the results you get in your life. Let thoughts of happiness, peace, and fulfillment empower your mind. Invite your mind to send up happy, peaceful, and fulfilling thoughts that will empower your life. Your thoughts are massive and powerful and control your destiny. Your predominant thoughts must be focused on and in harmony with all the good in your life; not what you don't have or don't want. Make a conscious effort, and you will develop the ability to focus the power of your thoughts on creating the life you desire and deserve. Ralph Waldo Emerson said that the only thing that can grow is that to which we give energy. So focus your energy on what you want, not what you don't want.

THE SUPER-CONSCIOUS

For centuries, the Super-Conscious has been studied and debated. Doctors, writers, and philosophers maintain it is an essential component to all success and accomplishment. Carl Jung was the first to refer to this Super-Conscious mind. What he discovered is that the collective wisdom and knowledge of all the ages was contained in this Super-

Conscious mind and was available to everyone. Ralph Waldo Emerson understood that all power and possibility, for the average person, came from using this mind on a regular basis. Also, Napoleon Hill, author of *Think and Grow Rich*, called this power the "Infinite Intelligence." He spent more than 20 years interviewing 25,000 people and 500 of the most successful men and women in America and concluded that, without exception, their ability to tap into this higher form of Infinite Intelligence was the primary reason for their great success in life.

YOU ARE ALWAYS CONNECTED TO THE INFINITE POWER AND INTELLIGENCE WHETHER YOU ARE CONSCIOUSLY AWARE OF IT OR NOT. WHEN YOU BECOME CONSCIOUS, YOU CAN USE THAT INTELLIGENCE TO ENHANCE YOUR LIFE AND THE LIVES OF OTHERS.

Whatever you choose to call it, this power is as available to you at this very minute as it ever has been to anyone, anywhere. In each one of us, we have access to this higher phase of mind and soul. The Super-Conscious doesn't have to be developed; it just needs to be recognized to use it effectively. Most of us experience the occasional bout of genius and unexplainable knowledge. Often it comes in the form of an idea that is from far beyond you. If you are tuned in you will realize that you are merely an instrument for the Infinite to express through you. Learn to become open to this form of communication. Allow yourself to honor those ideas that seem to come from somewhere outside of you. You are always connected to the Infinite Power and Intelligence whether you are consciously aware of it or not. When you become conscious, you can use that Intelligence to enhance your life and the lives of others around you.

It is not unusual for two people separated by thousands of miles to be thinking of each other at the same time. When you look at an Aspen tree and enjoy its splendor, you do not notice that beneath the ground are its roots that are connected to all the other Aspen trees around it. It is but one family connected with unique individual expressions. In this way, we are connected to each other and our source.

YOU HAVE DOMINION OVER YOUR OWN THOUGHTS. NO PERSON OR CIRCUMSTANCE CAN MAKE YOU CHOOSE WHAT YOU THINK ABOUT.

When you are well-attuned to another person, such as your spouse or mate, you will often have thoughts identical to him or her, at the same time during the day, and you will only find out that you had reached the same conclusion when you compare notes hours later. Or the phone may ring as you are reaching for it to make a call and the person on the line is the one you were just about to call. These are examples of your connection to the Super-Conscious mind at work. Often Rod and I open our mouths, at the same time, to express the same idea or realization. We love these moments for we recognize them as validation that we are always connected through the Infinite Intelligence. Unfortunately, most of us have been conditioned to ignore this or pass it off as coincidence. The problem is that if we continue to push these experiences off to the side, our ability to consciously tap into the Super-Conscious diminishes.

I'm sure you've heard the expression, "use it or lose it." Well it is true. It is important to notice synchronistic moments in your life and just acknowledge them as truth. Realize that this is the Infinite Intelligence, or Universe, speaking to you. Stay sharp to these and be open to them. Wonderful things happen around you every day. It is important to notice and grasp that this is how it is supposed to be. So often people tell me a story of synchronicity and they say, "Isn't that just weird?" No, it is not weird; it is how it is supposed to be. It is how it works. Give little thanks for these moments and stay open for more. Rod likes to say that these synchronistic moments are a validation that he is connected and on his right path.

Once you begin to recognize the existence of these new and unsuspected faculties, and validate them on a regular basis, soon they will filter over into your subconscious mind. The best things we have come from the Super-Conscious. It's the source of all examples of imagination and creativity. **Within the Super-Conscious mind is the functioning belief that anything is possible.** The Universe is yours for the asking. All great inventors tapped into this faculty. Success, art, music, love, and spiritual insight stem from this Infinite Power.

YOUR THOUGHTS ARE MASSIVE AND POWERFUL AND CONTROL YOUR DESTINY.

Any time you see, read, listen to, or experience a great achievement of any kind that touches something deep inside you, you are witness to a Super-Conscious creation. Have you ever had a thought about a product or service that you didn't act upon only to see it later? That thought that came to you came from the Super-Conscious mind and your subconscious mind stomped on it while the other person overcame their limiting beliefs.

THE SUPER-CONSCIOUS DOESN'T HAVE TO BE DEVELOPED; IT JUST NEEDS TO BE RECOGNIZED.

A great example is my nephew Geoff. He was in one of my classes where we were studying the book *Think and Grow Rich,* and as I was beginning to explain about the Super-Conscious mind, Geoff asked me the question, "Can thoughts come from somewhere outside yourself?" I said, "Absolutely, that's what we're talking about here, is our ability to tap into the Super-Conscious." Out of this class, Geoff opened his mind and asked the question, "What's needed?" When we're asking questions openly with this intention for an answer, that is actually what prayer is. At that moment, he created a timely and successful business based on the current need in Idaho. When he and his family decided to move to California, what seemed like a big risk to those around him, he felt confident because he was armed with the knowledge that the principles were in place that he could continue to ask the right questions, tap into the Infinite and be open to the answers.

Because of his willingness to ask what's needed now and listen, he's created a new business in California, despite the economic downturn. In literally a matter of a few months, Geoff created a solid business from nothing and it continues to grow day by day. When new ideas come to you, be open and accept them as they are a gift from the Super-Conscious. The more acceptance you give them, the more often you'll receive them and use this magnificent gift to propel you forward in life. It has access to data and ideas outside your own experience, because it actually lies outside your human mind. This is why it is called a form of Universal or Infinite Intelligence; it is also referred to as God and many other names.

An attitude of calm, confident expectation is like a beacon in tapping into the Super-Conscious mind. When you adopt this attitude and accept the Super-Conscious as real and you confidently believe that everything that is happening to you is moving you progressively toward the achievement of your desires, the possibilities are limitless. Developing an attitude of clarity and calmness unleashes your Super-Conscious abilities. You can create this state of being by simply acknowledging the existence of and your connection to the Super Conscious.

What I have found effective is to start in a quiet, comfortable place. For me, this is while I clean my horses' stalls. I know that may sound strange to you but, for me, it is the most peaceful place to be. I like the sound of the horses munching on their hay and swishing their tails. Another calm time is while I am out on my runs. Find the place that best suits you. So I begin by simply acknowledging who

I am in my truth; not how I am showing up but that I am one with the Universe, one with the One Mind, the Infinite Intelligence and I give thanks for this knowing. I continue on this path of acknowledgment and thanks and I begin to experience my spiritual self and my connection with all living things, visible and invisible. I soon experience that I am connected with the One and experience that the Infinite Intelligence does in fact work through me. I give thanks for the things I desire. It may be I desire clarity and calm. I give thanks for them. I continue on giving thanks for whatever it is I desire in my life: money, relationship, etc. I give thanks for the knowing that these things are mine now. I know that because there is no separation from Infinite Intelligence and me that all things are possible. <u>The clearer the desire and statement of knowing it is within you, the clearer the manifestation.</u>

I always end every session of what I call "Scientific Prayer" with the following:

"I give thanks for my Divine Right to choose my experience every moment of every day, and in this moment I choose, Love, Joy, Radiant Health, and Prosperity and I choose to express Love in all that I do and when I notice that I am not coming from this place of harmony and love, I simply choose again." This is an important last line because if I choose to express love in all that I do and then I find that I have gone into reaction or judgment about something or someone, it is easy to get out the old hammer and start beating myself up for not keeping my word about always coming from a loving place. This way, as soon as I notice, I simply say *"I choose again."*

As with your subconscious mind, when you think unlimited, exciting, and abundant thoughts, the Super-Conscious mind will accept your thoughts as a command and go to work to materialize them into your reality. In essence this is your prayer. This is the difference between successful and unsuccessful people. **Successful people think and talk about what they want, and unsuccessful people talk about what they don't want.** Listed below are a few simple suggestions to help you utilize the Super-Conscious power to get what you truly want in life.

> EITHER WE CHOOSE OUR THOUGHTS OR CHOOSE TO ALLOW OTHER'S THOUGHTS IN; EITHER WAY IT IS A CHOICE.

- Decide exactly what you want in life. Create the picture – Let your imagination run wild.

- Detail your goals and visions in writing. Always write your goals and visions in present tense. ("I give thanks for this is my life now." Or "I am so happy and grateful now that . . .") Speak in first-person with "I AM" and "I Have" statements.

- Visualize your new life repeatedly. As soon as you notice a picture that is not what you want, replace it with the picture of what you do want.

- Act as though the Super-Conscious mind were bringing your dreams into reality. When you know that you know, you will act as if – so how will you be acting in your life when you do have exactly what you want? Act that way now.

- Turn it over to the Infinite Power. Know that it is Done and Complete.
- Be grateful every moment for what is in your life and for what you know is in the process of manifesting itself. Be open and willing for it to be in your life now.

The Universe responds appropriately **at the level of your awareness** and **your willingness to grow and take action.** Choose the thoughts that support you in your quest for a healthy, happy, prosperous life. Life is miserable if you continue to live with the preconceived notions that keep you stuck. Your ideas or thoughts are your own choice. Either we choose our thoughts or choose to allow others' thoughts in; either way it is a *CHOICE*...... It is your choice.

CHAPTER 3
— GETTING OUT OF YOUR OWN WAY —

You are never given a wish without also being given the power to make it true.

–Richard Bach

3

CHAPTER

Our thoughts are the single most important factor contributing to our success in life. So whatever thoughts you allow to occupy your mind determine your results. In fact, you can look at the life you have right now and you'll see which thoughts you focus on the most. I spent several years feeling sorry for myself and punished everyone around me for the loss of my father. After returning to live with my mother, after my father's death, she moved us to Pacific Beach and boarded out my horse, Flame. The stable was quite a ways from our house, so I rarely was able to visit her. Flame was the only tangible piece of Daddy left, and when Mother wanted to sell her, I refused. I was treading water in life; even though I held on to my dream of a ranch and husband, I lost all belief in myself.

Angry at everyone and with my life, I pulled inward and separated myself from love. I watched my family go on with their lives and succeed. The more they moved forward the further I diminished. Along the way I made decisions about myself and others that would take real dedication and intention to undo in order to create the life I really wanted. This may sound familiar to some of you. You too may have made some decisions that have caused some emotional upheaval in your life.

The amount of love and money in your life, at this moment, is a reflection of your thoughts, more accurately, your deepest beliefs. Before I was able to allow love and financial success into my life, I first had to create the vision of these things in my mind. By changing the way I looked at myself and others, I was able to affect a change that would allow me to create a life of my choice. You may be wishing for romance and greater financial success; however, remember your predominate thoughts create your beliefs and, subsequently, these beliefs manifest into your reality.

THE AMOUNT OF LOVE AND MONEY IN YOUR LIFE AT THIS MOMENT IS A REFLECTION OF YOUR THOUGHTS.

You have the ability to control your thoughts. In truth, we all think in pictures. To prove my point, I'd like you to imagine your ideal life. Do you see a group of graphs and charts detailing how much money you have or a printout listing the qualities of your perfect mate? No, instead you likely picture a beautiful home filled with love and abundance.

So, what does your ideal life look like? Really let your mind wander. Dare to dream big. Ask the Universe for the answers. When you open your mind, what was once unachievable now is achievable and the right action to accomplish your desires will appear. Imagine every detail of what your ideal life looks like. Write down your thoughts as you visualize yourself living the life of your dreams *now, not in the future*. A helpful exercise for some people is to cut pictures out of magazines that most closely represent the life of their dreams. This can be helpful if you have a difficult

YOU CAN CREATE
THE LIFE OF
YOUR DREAMS
INTO A REALITY
IF YOU CAN
CREATE THE
VISION AND LIVE
IT IN YOUR MIND
AND HEART
EACH DAY.

time picturing what you want in your mind. It is important that you feel the emotion inside yourself as you imagine yourself in your new life. How do you feel living this life? Who have you become in order to create this life? Who have you attracted around you? You can create the life of your dreams into a reality if you can create the vision and live it in your mind and heart each day.

A dear friend of mine, Judi Kieffer, of Kieffer Design Group, demonstrated this process above so beautifully in her life by visualizing and staying clear of her dream. Judi was in one of the Mastermind groups I facilitated and also went through a Goal Achiever Program with me. She was also the interior designer on our resort home in Tamarack Resort. This is a story she was kind enough to share with us. She calls it *"Last Chance"*; I call it *"Learning to Wait For What Is"*. This is her story…..

"I dreamed of it for over 7 years. I knew what I wanted, what it would look like, smell like and what it felt like. I was so there. Now, I just had to find it and this day felt like my last chance. I had been dreaming of owning a cabin retreat in the mountains on many acres, large enough to watch my horses roam free in the swaying green, lush grasses with colorful wildflowers swaying in the soft breezes that only the mountain wilderness can provide. And large enough to have a cabin and horse barn where I could have huge barn doors at

both ends open up to the most beautiful views in either direction – sunset and sunrise, with just enough shadowing from the pine trees to embrace the lovely old structure made of reclaimed barn wood. Oh the stories it will tell me of past experiences and the new ones it will hold and share in its new life. The property would have a creek running through it and hundreds of acres and miles of forest land that would be my newfound backyard to ride my pasture buddies and enjoy my gratitude walks.

I had been looking for years, in all sorts of areas and places. Why couldn't I find it? Why was it taking so long, I wondered many times? I resisted and persisted and didn't know what I was doing wrong.

Craig and I had been seeing each other for 5 years at this point and often talked of sharing a property like this together. We both looked into our sources for properties and would take weekend road trips on occasion to McCall, Idaho. We would discover new places and visit our favorite places in New Meadows, Idaho, as well. We would drive up and down the same old roads and Craig would tell me stories of how he dreamed of someday owning the Old Circle C Ranch. I wanted to do more than drive those roads so I would show him listings I had cut out and would leave him voice messages of my finds. Craig was not as responsive as I would have liked him to be so I would get more anxious and persistent. 'I want to make this happen,' I would say, and the only way it would be is to be persistent, push and find it. (Little did I know it's all in the way it's presented . . . or not presented!).

Finally, on the 4th of July, 2006, Craig and I decided to spend the day in McCall and possibly look around at some properties – see what we could find. That day I shared with Craig that I talked to a mutual friend who is a knowledgeable real estate broker who specializes in land properties, Judy Land, of course, Jeri's sister. She could help us find that perfect piece of land. He was very reluctant and wasn't sure that we needed the help. I just remember Jeri sharing with me that involving others and networking will bring more power and success to the experience. So I reminded him of this, but he still wasn't convinced, but there wasn't a 'NO'. We agreed to just talk more about the business agreement for starters. So I took that 'crack in the door' and flung it wide open! I asked Judy to send some listings for starters to just see what was out there.

I guess that might have been a little too much too fast and too controlling . . . it was 'all over but the crying', so to speak. He wanted to have a meeting, take it slow, make a certain agreement that worked for everyone – but I was already down the first stretch, around the bend without a saddle – no need. (Figuratively speaking!)

In his supportive way he made it clear that I was just so eager to take charge and control of the situation. Well, yes, that would be me; but as I saw it and I said, 'I only jump in when you don't step up to the plate and take charge. I would gladly support you and encourage you doing this if you wish.' Wow that was a big discussion and very grounding for both of us.

So we decided to go for a drive to our favorite spots in New Meadows, and just see what we would find, and also enjoy a hike and talk about things. There was still a little tension in the air as we turned into the 'Last Chance' turn off of Hwy 55, and to our destination.

The hike was beautiful and the weather was perfect. I personally decided in my quiet space to remember words that Jeri had shared with me – 'to not resist but just be there in love and let the other person have their space to freely talk openly – no judgment. Receive the words and love them through it all.'

HOLD YOUR VISION CLEARLY AND FEEL WHAT IT FEELS LIKE TO BE LIVING THAT LIFE IN EVERY WAY.

So I decided to just BE and listen. Upon listening and not resisting – (although difficult at times, especially when I thought it was the Last Chance Craig and I were going to have to make this work in buying a property together), he finally asked for my support in letting him lead the way to find the property together for us. That was really hard to relinquish that control – wow, I had to gulp it down. I really felt like the growth that Craig and I had experienced and what I had personally discovered was presenting itself in a whole new light. I actually felt very at peace and all the heavy load was lifted when we embraced this meeting of the minds.

From here on out is the storybook ending – we left the hike out of Last Chance turn off, drove down our favorite road – but didn't see any signs. So we enjoyed the ride and the rest of the weekend. On Monday, Judy had sent us an email with numerous listings. Craig called me and said, 'Did you read Judy's email yet?Look at the third listing – it's on Fish Lake Road.' Craig's favorite road and the one we drove up all the time. It just so happens that this sign was there on the road but we just didn't go far enough. Craig said, 'Wow, I guess we should hire Judy!" He was clear now. So we made the trip to McCall that next weekend.

I didn't know what to think and I hadn't seen this property before. All I remember is the long, slow, bumpy drive down the road as I was talking to God, and I said, 'I just hope this is going to be everything we have been dreaming of and wanting.' And a very clear voice said to me, 'More than you can imagine.'

So needless to say the rest is history and amazing. The journey in life can be amazing if we are ready to release and receive and trust in the glory of God's Divine Power. Many times our dreams come to us through other people and being open to this experience can show you glorious moments.

Jeri has been a true blessing and white light in my journey. She has and will continue to be a beautiful friend, mentor and inspiration in my world. I am grateful to her for showing me how

WHEN YOU OPEN YOUR MIND, WHAT WAS ONCE UNACHIEVABLE IS NOW EASILY DONE WHEN YOU TAKE THE RIGHT ACTION.

to love more deeply and empower others and myself by just letting go.

That Last Chance trip could have been Craig's and my last chance to make this work together – but we chose differently! You see, thanks to Jeri and Rod they have opened the door for us to 'choose in' to experiencing ourselves more fully and to always come from a loving place, no matter what the situation or position. If they had not suggested the PSI Seminars work, Jeri's classes, and the many very supportive talks and insights that they have shared with both of us over the years, our lives would be very different right now."

-Judi Kieffer

Judi and Craig did buy that property together, 40 acres. As I pointed out to Judi, it really wasn't their last chance, though it felt like it to her. She was just learning to wait for what is. Her vision was clear; it was just the details to be worked out. There is a gestation period we must learn to accept. When we are fully ready to accept our good, it will manifest itself.

There are many lessons in this story. Judi runs a very successful business. She has developed her way of doing things and, for the most

YOUR OLD PATTERNS MAY BRING YOU LIMITED SUCCESS BUT THERE IS MORE WAITING FOR YOU WHEN YOU ARE WILLING TO LET GO AND LET THE POWER OF THE UNIVERSE SHOW YOU THE WAY.

part, it has worked for her. She is passionate and assertive. She is always positive and has boundless energy, but even with all of this, she was not able to "make this happen". She had to become open to the possibility that there was another way, and most importantly, be willing to surrender to it. When Judi got out of the way, the way opened fully to her.

BECOME OPEN TO THE POSSIBILITY THAT THERE IS ANOTHER WAY, AND MOST IMPORTANTLY, BE WILLING TO SURRENDER TO IT.

Judi asked me why it took so long for her to create this ranch in her life when she had wanted it for so long. When we are in a state of wanting, that is what we are essentially praying for, the wanting. She said she wanted it and didn't want to wait any longer. The subconscious mind does not hear "not", as in, "did not want to wait"; it hears "want to wait". Again, we cannot force things to happen. We can only get clarity of that which we wish to create. We need to hold the vision clearly and feel what it feels like to be living that life in every way. We then let go of the outcome and be willing to do whatever shows up in front of us to do. When we are in alignment with the Universe, things seem to fall into place with ease. This doesn't mean that there is not a lot to do. There is plenty to do but it is not a struggle. We just do what is next for us to do, holding true to our vision of that which we choose to create. Always ask the question, "**Who do I need to become to create this in my life?**" We do have to shift in order to create something new and different than we have right now.

How many times in your life have you gotten in your own way of having what you want because you insist on doing it a certain way? You simply get stuck in your old patterns and stay committed to them, instead of being open to another way of looking at things. Your old patterns may bring you limited success but there is more waiting for you when you are willing to let go and let the power of the Universe show you the way.

CHAPTER 4

— YOUR LIFE BEYOND THE FIVE SENSES —

Most people do not fail because they aimed too high and missed; no, they fail because they aimed too low and hit.

–Les Brown

4

CHAPTER

There are definite steps you can take to intentionally create the results that you desire. We are all born with five senses: the ability to see, hear, smell, taste, and touch the world around us. By the age of five most children have a complete understanding of their ability to use their five senses, and to understand the world and environment around them through these senses. **The five senses are limited to telling us and showing us what already "is". They have no power to create or transform.**

Intellectual skills, however, do have the power to create and transform your habits. Before you can harness their power, you first need to take stock of where you are in your life. It is important to see how you not only view yourself but how you view others as well. A great example might be if you find yourself being jealous or judgmental of a co-worker. You like to think that you have these thoughts because you are clear that you do not want to be like that person, yet the simple reaction that you experience to their behavior puts more focus on that behavior and attracts more of the same to you. In truth, the feelings and reactions

> IT IS IMPORTANT TO SEE HOW YOU NOT ONLY VIEW YOURSELF BUT HOW YOU VIEW OTHERS AS WELL.

you have to that co-worker <u>all</u> reside inside of you and, if you are listening, they are teaching you that within yourself is the only place where change can occur, not outside. Focusing on others' behavior can inhibit you from focusing on what you want in *your* life. Conversely, by living with the thought process that each one of us, including your co-worker, deserves happiness and you embrace life with an attitude of gratitude and prosperity, a life of abundance awaits you.

FOCUSING ON OTHERS BEHAVIOR CAN INHIBIT YOU FROM FOCUSING ON WHAT YOU WANT IN YOUR LIFE.

Again, it is important to understand and appreciate that everything happens inside of you. For example, <u>when you meet someone whose qualities you admire, it would be impossible for you to recognize those qualities if they were not already inside of you</u>. Understanding what I have just said is so important to your future success and happiness. Read it again.

It is imperative that you find that place in your heart to truly bless and be excited for those who are successful in life. I cannot tell you how important this also is. Conversely, bless those who are not. They are not bad or wrong; they simply do not know a different or better way. We all do the best we know how, at any point in time based on our level of awareness and our willingness to grow. Notice, I did not say *we do the best we can*; I said *we do the best we know how*. We can always do better but the challenge is learning how. A great place to start is by forgiving yourself for your past and moving forward from this point. This may be just forgiving yourself for not having the life you desire. And again, start

WHEN YOU MEET SOMEONE WHOSE QUALITIES YOU ADMIRE, IT WOULD BE IMPOSSIBLE FOR YOU TO RECOGNIZE THOSE QUALITIES IF THEY WERE NOT ALREADY INSIDE OF YOU.

genuinely being excited for other people's good fortune. As an example, when you see someone who has something you wish you had, you can say to yourself, "*I don't know your story or how you developed the money and relationship-consciousness to have what you have in your life, but good for you*". This is a good place to start.

The great news is that you can consciously create the life you want for yourself; you can actually learn to develop your intellectual faculties. These are necessary to develop in order to start taking charge of the thoughts you hold in your mind. Most people do not even know what their Intellectual Faculties are. I am going to teach you what they are so that you can begin working on developing them right away. Doing so is an important step in the right direction. It will, however, require discipline on your part to work with and develop them on a daily basis. So, what are these Intellectual Faculties and how do you develop them?

There are six; they are:

1. Intuition
2. Imagination
3. Perception
4. Focus
5. Memory
6. Reason

These six Intellectual Faculties are so important that we're going to discuss each one individually. The first one, *Intuition,* has guided me through life on many occasions. Wayne Dyer says that, "if prayer is us speaking to God, then Intuition is when God is speaking to us." This is a powerful statement that demonstrates intuition so beautifully. You know when you get that great idea that seems to come from nowhere; it just appears out of nowhere into your mind? That is your Intuition or God speaking to you.

You must learn to trust your Intuition in order to move beyond your current level of operation. How many times in your life has there been a situation that you "just knew" something and you didn't listen to your knowing and later you said, "I should have listened to my instinct"? Yes, that was your intuitive faculty at work. You must learn to trust it. As you trust it and use it, you will develop it. Another example of Intuition is the connection we have with other people. When someone says something to you and you see their lips moving and the words coming out of their mouth but you "just know" they mean something else – yes, this is your intuitive faculty at work as well.

IT IS IMPERATIVE THAT YOU FIND THAT PLACE IN YOUR HEART TO TRULY BLESS AND BE EXCITED FOR THOSE WHO ARE SUCCESSFUL IN LIFE.

It works both ways, by the way. When you speak to someone and you are not fully truthful, they know too. I've repeated one of my favorite quotes by Ralph Waldo Emerson for many years: ***Who you are speaks so loudly, I cannot hear the words you say.*** This is a powerful statement of our intuitive nature. In thousands of ways over the course of a day, you teach people about the kind of person you are. Learn to trust yourself and that translates to how others treat you. We know what is in people's hearts regardless of what they may say. We know when others are being authentic or not; and they also know this about us. You see, we really are connected.

Imagination is our creative side and when we blend *Imagination with Intuition* this is our God-like self. It is said that we are made in the image and likeness of God; well this is the way in which we are created in this image and likeness. Life is ever expressing and expanding. We are co-creators in our life and have this urge built into us to co-create, to express who we are fully and expand our consciousness. We must do this or we decay. It is a law. We cannot deny this part of our nature. When we neglect it, there is a price to pay. So be courageous with this and dream big. Most of us have not really exercised our Imagination since we were in the sandbox as a young child. Honor and embrace this side of yourself. Go ahead, be courageous and wild. How do you really want your life to look?

WHEN WE BEGIN TO CHANGE THE WAY WE LOOK AT THINGS, THE THINGS WE LOOK AT BEGIN TO CHANGE.

Next is *Perception*. This is simply our point of view. We need to develop it so that we can perceive things differently than we currently do. If you can not perceive words, behaviors, actions, thoughts, or life in general differently then you will always create the same results. Wayne Dyer says, "When we begin to change the way we look at things, the things we look at begin to change." This is so powerful.

An example of how we can see things differently is to think about when you have fallen in love with someone. You know that amazing feeling of being in love. Maybe you went on your first date with someone you have wanted to be with for a long time and on the date you find out that they too wanted to be with you. You express your feelings for each other and you know this is the beginning of a wonderful relationship. The next day you leave home and head for work feeling like a million bucks. You look around and everything looks so bright and beautiful. Nothing bothers you that day. Everything is hopeful and wonderful. All you have done is change the way you look at the world. You changed your *Perception*. This is a skill you want to develop so that you can call upon it and use it with intention while you are creating your new life.

Focus is your ability to hold your attention and thoughts on something. An example would be the use of a magnifying glass with the sun. If you were to move the magnifying glass back and forth on different views over a piece of paper, it will do nothing. Yet, if you hold it still and focus the beam of light to a fixed point on the paper, the sun burns the paper in seconds; this is how you must learn to use your *Focus*. Like that focused beam of light on the paper, you can learn to focus on the vision you have set for yourself. You must not let anything distract you. Some call this "WILL" but where there is a WILL there is a WALL. **We cannot force life to be the way we want it. We can, however, create vision and become in harmony with it.**

YOU CAN CONSCIOUSLY CREATE THE LIFE YOU WANT FOR YOURSELF.

Next is *Memory*. Memory is two parts; there are our memories and then there is the act of remembering. We all have a perfect Memory; it is just under-developed. Never say again that you do not have a good Memory because you are conditioning your mind to believe this which reinforces the thought. It will give you what you ask for every time, whether you like it or not.

Your Memory is there to support you in everything you do. All you need to know about your Memory is to use it to support yourself in having what you say you want in your life. When challenged, call up your good experiences to encourage yourself to keep going. When discouraging thoughts surface, welcome them first and then see if you would be willing to let them go. If so, replace them right away with good Memories; Memories of you succeeding in life. It might be helpful to write down the wins in your life. This can be as simple as remembering when you were kind to someone and you felt you made a difference.

IF YOU HAVE RECEIVED AN IDEA, YOU ARE CAPABLE OF ACHIEVING IT.

Lastly is *Reason*. When used properly, *Reason* will help you in selecting the thoughts that you allow to linger in your conscious mind and it will help you during your planning process of reaching for your dreams. What you *do not* want to do is let *Reason* talk you out of a great idea just because it is unfamiliar and scary to you. Remember when you have had that great idea and then the next thought was, *"Silly you; who do you think you are dreaming of that? There is no way you can do that. What are you thinking?"* We have all done this at some point in our lives and I am here to tell you, *never* buy into that again. I want you to know that if you received the idea, you are capable of achieving it. If you were not, you would never have had that idea. So never let Reason work in the wrong way again by talking you out of your dreams. Instead, use your reasoning skills to pass judgment on the thoughts you allow to linger in your conscious mind. Are they thoughts that support you in achieving your dreams or are they suppressive?

In summary, when your *Intuition* is at work and you have a great idea, be grateful for it and ask these questions: if I act on this idea, will it move me in the direction of my dream? Will it move me into more of the person I am meant to be? If you can answer yes to either of these questions, you must act, you must move on it right away. Let your *Imagination* work it up into an elaborate dream, *Perceive* it as it will be when it is accomplished, hold that vision and Focus on it using your *Memories* to support you and then let *Reason* help you with your plans to get you there. And get moving!

You then must give yourself permission to dream; dream as big as you can. Does your dream give you a sense of aliveness? Do you need the help of a higher power to get you there? If not, this dream may not be big enough for you. Who do you want to be? What do you want to accomplish? Use your Imagination to work up the dream into a clarity that is so real it is tangible. See yourself being that person. How are you dressed? Who are the people you have attracted to you? What kind of home are you living in? How are you seen in your community? How do you contribute to others? See yourself providing a great service in your chosen career or business. Allow your *intuitive* nature to work with you and your *Imagination*. This is you co-creating. This is a time for courage. Give yourself permission to dream big.

Take your time with this process. You will find as you keep at this your vision will expand and clarify. It is important for you to know who you were meant to be. What is your real purpose here? What truly fulfills you? You may be familiar with a great personal development teacher by the name of Tony Robbins. He explains in his Ultimate Relationship Course that we all have 6 basic needs. The first four are more like personality needs. They are superficial yet we will do anything to have them met. They are our need for <u>certainty</u>, <u>uncertainty</u> or variety, the need for <u>love or connection</u> and the need for <u>significance</u>. We will either have these needs met in a positive way or a negative way but we will have these needs met one way or another. There are two more, as I mentioned, and these two needs when focused upon and created will automatically fill the first four needs. These two needs are our need for <u>personal growth</u> and <u>contribution</u>. As we focus our lives on our personal growth and contributing to others we fulfill all our needs and we may just be on to discovering our true purpose on the planet.

Tony's work is brilliant when working with intimate relationships on understanding the needs of your partner and how to fill them. This work of course spans all relationships and it serves to ground us in our knowing of self.

WILLINGNESS

Something so critical to your success, not mentioned above, is Willingness. Willingness is harder to describe because it is more a spiritual concept. The Intellectual Faculties can be practiced and measured each day. Willingness, however, comes from within and is based upon your personal sense of worthiness. Actually practice willingness by using these words when you want something big in your life: "I am willing to have this happen." Listen intently to the inner voice after thinking these words and notice the perspective or energy of that inner voice. Your inner voice may be silent in full acceptance that you are in harmony with the Universe and know that you are on your way to achieving what you want. On the other hand, your inner voice may become animated and tell you why you can't have what you want. That inner voice may be very reasonable and convincing; however, it's essential to realize that this inner voice may not be authentically yours but rather deep-seated thoughts and beliefs, poured in by others in your formative life that you, along the way, never questioned until now. Well, question them and ask yourself if they are true. Oftentimes, that inner voice will be telling you that you are not worthy of what you say you want. It is at this point in time you will

AS WE FOCUS OUR LIVES ON OUR PERSONAL GROWTH AND CONTRIBUTING TO OTHERS WE FULFILL ALL OUR NEEDS AND WE MAY JUST BE ON TO DISCOVERING OUR TRUE PURPOSE ON THE PLANET.

have to examine your Willingness to have all the things in your life that you say you want. Just stay with this. By the time you complete this book, you'll find your truth and realize that you are deserving of all you desire. As a result of this shift, you will then gain the ability to declare your Willingness to create the life you want and take action to make it into reality.

CHAPTER 5
— A NEW UNDERSTANDING OF
THE LAWS WE NEVER BREAK —

Miracles come in moments.
Be ready and willing.

–Wayne Dyer

5

CHAPTER

Your underlying consciousness, often referred to as your subconscious mind, now here referred to as your "auto-pilot", is always on, even when you are not. A great example of this is when you are driving your car on a long stretch and you notice you can't recall the drive because your thoughts were elsewhere. Who drove that car? Consider this: the same unconscious consciousness that drove the car is in control of a great deal of your behavior and what you attract into your life. If this is true, and you intuitively know it is, then it might be useful to become aware of the inherited and created underlying thoughts that make up your auto-pilot.

YOUR SURROUNDINGS TEACH YOU A LOT ABOUT YOUR STATE OF MIND.

By doing so, you can develop further your ability to get into true partnership with it and change the results and surroundings in your life to look more like what you say you want. Just stop and consider, for a moment, your surroundings. In this case, we define surroundings as the circumstances and conditions you have created and attracted into your life. Where you live, what kind of car you drive, how you present yourself with clothes, hair, makeup (if applicable), what type of job you have, what type of relationships you have, where you hang out, what your friends are like, what your hobbies are, how much money you have, etc. etc. All these expressions that make up your surroundings actually represent the underlying consciousness that is running you most of the time. How many times have you expressed, 'This is me, this is just the way I am," when someone has questioned you about your surroundings? In truth, your surroundings teach you a lot about your state of mind, **up to now.** This is not good or bad, it is just what is and you can do something about it when you become aware of what makes up your auto-pilot.

What works about the auto-pilot metaphor is that in an airplane, the auto-pilot controls the speed and direction the plane travels. So, too, our auto-pilot, our underlying consciousness, or subconscious mind, is constantly setting the speed and direction of our life. You are the one who sets the course and the auto-pilot takes you on a course based upon prior beliefs.

Different than the auto-pilot in a plane, your auto-pilot also is a great attractor, attracting events and circumstances based upon the formulas you have both inherited and consciously poured into yourself. When you get that, and when you stop blaming others for your surroundings, life as it was truly meant to be experienced begins. So the next time you wake up, stumble to the shower, shave or put on makeup, just stop and become aware of your surroundings. Take them in, be grateful for what you have created and ask yourself if you want to change any of it and if so, what parts.

Staying in auto-pilot mode may seem like the easy road to take but it keeps you stuck moving in a direction that is not of your conscious choosing. Your life becomes a reaction to all of your circumstances. Your underlying consciousness is doing exactly what you have given it permission to do. It keeps you in the familiar and controlled through your internal voice that incessantly speaks to you, especially when you try to break out and create some new behaviors. Your auto-pilot wants to keep you in what seems familiar, safe and right. Notice that you will defend your position and fight to stay in familiar territory where you feel safe; even if it looks tumultuous, it is what is familiar to you.

For example:

You've seen or heard of someone who, while growing up, is mistreated at home and they wind up marrying someone who also mistreats them, or they themselves mistreat their children or relationship partner. It is not that they like or want it; it is just that it is familiar to them and it is what they have come to expect.

On the other hand, if someone is praised as they are growing up, they tend to praise others and they also tend to attract relationships that are more supportive. Again, it is what is familiar to them.

If you think about it, if you truly understand that you actually can reset your course and have ultimate power over what you attract to you, how much easier life would be. You would have discovered consciously the secret formula that you choose the thoughts that program the subconscious mind that cause you to show up and behave the way you do. Your subconscious mind does what it has always done; it keeps evolving based on the new thoughts that you hand over to it. This is what true growth is all about.

That part of you that is the _observer_ is your authentic self. The other part of your authentic self is you as the _chooser_. The observer is completely detached from the auto-pilot and in those moments of awareness can choose to reset the course. Like the air we can't see yet thrive from its gifts, so too your subconscious mind accepts without question what you put into it. You will likely experience resistance within yourself; however, it's in the DNA of your subconscious to listen, accept and respond to the thoughts you provide. That is why repetition of thought and prayer are important. The resistance will ultimately subside because your auto-pilot now begins to accept that you really want what you are asking for and will reprogram itself to give you what you say you want now. It is used to this behavior; you just may not have realized it.

> YOU ARE THE ONE THAT SETS THE COURSE AND THE AUTO PILOT TAKES YOU ON A COURSE BASED UPON PRIOR BELIEFS.

So what happens when you are in the in-between state of resetting your course? You will call upon your own internal faith. You will practice the Intellectual Faculties that we discussed in chapter 4. It is especially important to focus and hold your vision because the results you so desire may not just magically show up. Just as in the physical plane, there are laws at work. When you plant the seed, the seed must be given water and nutrients in order to gestate and become what it is meant to be. So too, your seeded thoughts must be watered and nurtured with your faith, trust and love of self for the underlying consciousness to do its job

> BE GRATEFUL FOR WHAT YOU HAVE CREATED AND ASK YOURSELF IF YOU WANT TO CHANGE ANY OF IT AND IF SO, WHAT PARTS.

of serving you. If you reintroduce your old thoughts and beliefs and listen to your old internal voices, it's like putting contaminants in your soil. No one else will take care of your soil better than you so stop expecting others to be the source of your happiness and growth. If you do so, you will realize that you have always known what is best for you and that you deserve your authentic life, a life that you consciously design. You will begin to minimize the past behaviors that, while technically made by you, were actually driven on auto-pilot by the thoughts and influence of others in your formative years.

As you read through this book, I want you to keep your mind and heart open to new ways of thinking. I want to encourage you to push forward rather than fall back to that which seems more familiar. Whether the desire is a new career, your own business or a new relationship, including redefining the one you are in, you simply need to see what you want, welcome the internal resistance (if any), for that's the subconscious mind's job to keep you safe and familiar, and then give your mind permission to accept your new thoughts and move forward in joyous expectancy.

It is possible to have all that you want in this lifetime. You are a boundless, energetic being capable of doing anything and everything that your heart desires. Our abilities stretch far beyond the confines of our physical beings. Old and outdated thought processes can cloud our sight. We all have great power within us, yet we often operate on the physical plane trying to use logic where imagination would better serve us. Many of us are eager to have the support of the Universe, and yet we continue to plow along being stuck in the soil of old ideas that were poured in and wonder why nothing has changed. It is my desire to help you move away from struggle and more easily create the results you want in your life. Endless possibilities lie ahead once you shatter the illusions created by the preconceived notions of yourself and others. Remember, whatever your dream is, assuming it doesn't harm anyone, it has no right or wrong.

MOVING BEYOND THE PHYSICAL PLANE

As the laws of the mechanical Universe exist, so do the Laws of the Universe that govern and enhance our experience of self. One of the purposes of *"Where's The Love & Who's Got My Money?"* is to share with you these laws. You may not be aware of them, or may not have a full understanding of them. These are very precise laws that we all live by whether we know it or not. There are no exceptions to these laws. They apply to all living things at all times. They apply to each of us whether we are aware of them or not. So it is important to gain a better understanding of how they work. Let me ask you this. If you throw an apple into the air, where does it go? Simple, it falls back to the ground. This is the Law of Gravity. You can't see gravity yet you know it exists by your experience

YOUR UNDERLYING CONSCIOUSNESS IS DOING EXACTLY WHAT YOU HAVE GIVEN IT PERMISSION TO DO.

of it. So too it is with the spiritual laws. Just as there is a Law of Gravity, the Laws of the Universe are working in your life, at all times.

What do you believe would happen if you didn't have a good understanding of how the Law of Gravity works and used it incorrectly? Lacking the understanding of what goes up must come down can be disastrous. Everything in our Universe is governed by unwavering laws. As you understand the importance of living in harmony with these laws, you'll soon find fulfillment, not only in your finances and relationships, but in all areas of your life.

The Universal Laws are all interconnected and operate inter-dependently with each other. Everything in the Universe is energy. At the microscopic level, you and I are nothing more than a glob of electrons spinning fervently. Once we act in accordance with these laws, our physical, mental, spiritual, and emotional growth flourishes because we're following the flow of the currents that build and maintain all of creation.

In the words of great teacher, Dr. Harry Morgan Moses of Spirit Works Center in Southern California, *"The more disciplined you are in connecting with this energy, the more "lightened" you become. Love has the ability to break through and transform your outmoded beliefs and "old stuff". It infuses the "rocky soil of the mind" with living energy, making it more fertile to receive and Be Love! Creation of good is a natural result."*

Since all of our thoughts, feelings, words, and actions are all forms of energy, they vibrate back to us to create our realities. Energy moves in a circle, so the combined thoughts, feelings, words and actions of everyone on the planet create our collective consciousness. In order to create a world of prosperity and abundance for our entire Universe, it is essential to alter our thoughts and emotions. A full understanding of the Universal Laws helps you to do so.

> YOUR SUBCONSCIOUS MIND DOES WHAT IT HAS ALWAYS DONE; IT KEEPS EVOLVING BASED ON THE NEW THOUGHTS THAT YOU HAND OVER TO IT.

- The Law of Attraction. Like attracts like and what you send out into the Universe you will receive in return. This refers to our thoughts and beliefs. Realize though that the thought is only the spark. You have to take action. Everything outside yourself is merely a reflection of you and where you are grounded in your belief systems.

- The Law of Vibration. Just as the waves of a pebble tossed into a pond vibrate outward, so do our thoughts, words, and feelings. Everything has its own vibrational frequency, unique unto itself. When we are vibrating at a high or positive energy we attract others of high energy. When we are in a low or negative energy we attract others who vibrate at that energy as well.

- The Law of Divine Oneness. Everything in the Universe is connected. Just accept this to be true – it is. Everything we do, think, say and believe affects others and the Universe around us. PSI Seminars has

> LIKE THE AIR
> WE CAN'T SEE
> YET THRIVE
> FROM ITS GIFTS,
> SO TOO YOUR
> SUBCONSCIOUS
> MIND, YOUR AUTO
> PILOT, ACCEPTS
> WITHOUT
> QUESTION WHAT
> YOU PUT INTO IT.

a wonderful mission statement, "World Peace one mind at a time", which accentuates this point. I have found PSI Seminars to have an incredible set of courses to understand and transform what is in your soil and to have a true experience of this truth of connection.

• The Law of Action. In order for your dreams to manifest, you have to first take action. It will start with a thought that will lead to an inspiration – act on it! I have a favorite saying here – **"When you are praying for potatoes, reach for a hoe."** Engage in actions that support your dreams. Don't be afraid if it is hard. You can handle hard. If it were easy, everyone would do it.

• The Law of Correspondence. This law explains that the physical world corresponds with all in the Universe, both visible and invisible. "As is above, So it is below". As a man thinketh in his heart so it is.

• The Law of Gestation. Just as a seed needs time to grow, everything in the Universe needs its own time of gestation. As you learn to ask for what you want, it is important to understand that you also have to prepare yourself by moving forward and trusting whatever the Universe puts in front of you. Be patient with yourself and keep holding your thoughts of belief and faith that what you desire is coming to you. When you are ready to receive your good, you shall.

- The Law of Cause and Effect. Every action has a consequence. You reap what you sow. Be clear that _cause_ starts with your _thoughts_ and _beliefs_; your _actions are effect_ and _they create your results_. Often people think that action was the cause that had an effect. The distinction I'm making here is that the thoughts and beliefs that you hold are the cause of the actions that you take. In other words, it is the effect of the thought and then the action creates the result. For instance, if you think and believe that the opposite sex cannot be trusted then your actions are cautious, withdrawn or even aggressive. The results you get in turn validate your beliefs. Conversely, if you view the opposite sex as trustworthy, your actions will be more open and giving, and so too your results will validate your beliefs.

- The Law of Compensation. Givers gain. Truly give of yourself emotionally, physically and financially and your gain can look any way you wish that fulfills your life. With regards to money, you get exactly what you are worth. If you want more money, create more value and if you want more love, give more love.

- The Law of Perpetual Transmutation of Energy. Wow, what a mouthful. I bet you were just thinking that. Each one of us and the world around us is constantly changing and in motion. Where we cannot control some of the changes surrounding us, we can however control how we change. **It is up to you to direct your change if you want greater results.**

- The Law of Relativity. This law helps us put our lives into perspective. No matter how we perceive our situation, there is always someone who is in a worse or better position. It is all relative. I would not appreciate the relationship I have with Rod had I not had some of the others in the past. So welcome the difference and diversity.

WHEN YOU PLANT THE SEED, THE SEED MUST BE GIVEN WATER AND NUTRIENTS IN ORDER TO GESTATE AND BECOME WHAT IT IS MEANT TO BE.

- The Law of Polarity. Everything is on a continuum and has an opposite. This law brings excitement and passion with it in an intimate relationship and it balances all things in the world. If everything and everyone were the same, it would all be very boring, wouldn't it?

- The Law of Rhythm. Everything vibrates and moves to certain rhythms which in turn establishes seasons, stages of growth and development, and cycles in life. Be conscious of the rhythms in the decades of your life. They can be a wonderful change. Embrace the evolution.

- The Law of Gender. Everything has its masculine (yang) and feminine (yin) principles, and these are the basis for all creation.

- The Law of Gratitude. All situations, whether you perceive them to be either good or bad, bring us gifts. It is difficult to let go unless you have an appreciation for what has happened. When you are grateful for both what you like and what you don't like you're able to let go and live in peace. Give thanks every day for all your gifts, especially those that show up as challenges.

These Universal Laws cannot be broken and work regardless of circumstance and situations. They work whether you believe in them or not. If you accept them as truth and work with them, then you will be the scientist and the world your lab. You need only learn the ways of the laws that will unlock your ability to connect with them in a way that works all the time, every time.

YOUR DIVINE RIGHT

Far too many of us do not believe that it is our Divine Right to have all that the Universe has to offer. I, too, at one time, felt this way about my happiness. After my Daddy died, I wanted to die too. I couldn't understand how this person, who I truly loved, could be taken from me. It wasn't until I really began to study and understand the Laws of the Universe that I realized that I was created with a purpose and deserved fulfillment. All events in my life were preparing me to become who I am today. They were my gifts, teaching me about life, and love and contribution.

> YOU ARE A BOUNDLESS ENERGETIC BEING CAPABLE OF DOING ANYTHING AND EVERYTHING THAT YOUR HEART DESIRES.

Along the way of my path, I discovered that I was also getting myself ready for an everlasting love in my life. Just like I chased money, I had been chasing the elusive relationship. I kept attracting relationships that couldn't last. Again, I had to see and hold myself in a different light in order to have a man in my life who would cherish me. To me, relationship and money are connected. Yes, I know there are people who have figured out how to make money who have not created relationships and people who seem to be happy in their relationships who have not created much money in their life. I still say the principles are the same and I wanted both. To me one without the other was not my idea of success. For me, and I think for most people, especially women, figuring out the money barrier first is important. Contrary to my upbringing where girls were taught that marriage was the key to their financial security and happiness, I do not think I could have gone into a healthy relationship if I had not proven to myself that I could make it on my own. So I chose to give myself everything I thought a man should give me. Notice the word "should" here. That may very well have been my thought process back then. Perhaps this is one of the reasons I couldn't seem to create the love of my life at that time.

ENDLESS POSSIBILITIES LIE AHEAD ONCE YOU SHATTER THE ILLUSIONS CREATED BY THE PRECONCEIVED NOTIONS OF YOURSELF AND OTHERS.

When we impose "should" on people they usually do not respond well to that. So I decided to shower myself with all the things I dreamed of coming from the man in my life. I had nice clothes, a big diamond ring, I drove the Mark series of the Lincoln Continental; I had a Mark III, a Mark IV and Mark V. The ultimate gift for me was when I created a ranch in the country where I could have my horses with me, my dogs and the whole country life.

I always dreamed of meeting a man with the same dream and we would go together in search of our dream home in the country. With the very limited time I had to date, working full-time in real estate, studying for my brokers' license and studying metaphysics, I noticed that the men I attracted saw me as I was showing up, as a businesswoman, successful and single in the city. When I shared my dream of living in the country on a ranch with my animals they looked at me in disbelief and would even say that this could not possibly be my idea of a dream life. It didn't seem to fit the picture they saw of me. So I decided that was good feedback and I needed to choose clearly all that I wanted and create that life on my own.

I went in search on my own and found the perfect home in the country and bought it. It was a most exciting time in my life. I knew that if I was going to attract the man of my dreams I needed to live the life of my dreams so he could see the whole picture. So now I had everything that I dreamed of, up to that point, except the loving husband and family of my own. In essence, I nurtured my soil and created a home for my new family to manifest. Your path will surely look very different, but the principles are the same. What do you want? How would you describe your dream life, career, and relationship?

I'm sure it was a bit strange for my married neighbors when this young, single woman moved into the neighborhood but I was on my mission to fill my house with a family. It really didn't take very long after that. I once again sat myself down and began clearing through the old cobwebs of misguided beliefs about myself and relationships. I wrote down all the things that were really important to me in my future husband starting with the most important one for me, a great friend. I wanted a friend, someone to cherish me, someone who was willing to look at his own stuff and work through it. I wasn't looking for someone without stuff, we all have stuff. I figured even if I could find someone without stuff he wouldn't have any interest in me anyway. No, I wanted a partner who was willing to be with me with my stuff too and love me through it; someone who was willing to assist me through my process in life as I was willing to assist him. I became very clear about what I wanted: a best friend and a family. As the Power works, he showed up with a readymade family. They all moved in with the dog too. Hmmmm. Be sure you know what you're praying for. You just might get it.

> IN ORDER TO CREATE A WORLD OF PROSPERITY AND ABUNDANCE FOR OUR ENTIRE UNIVERSE, IT IS ESSENTIAL TO ALTER OUR THOUGHTS AND EMOTIONS.

I met Rod and his two sons briefly at a circus I attended with my sister Judy, niece Tahnee and nephew Neal. Rod and his boys were friends with my sister Judy and her kids. We only had a short time to talk to each other but it was a memorable conversation. He really seemed so interesting. So different than other men I had spoken with. I really didn't think much about him in a relationship kind of way. I was dating someone else at the time and just didn't think about it. I just remember thinking he was an interesting guy.

As the Law of Gestation states, everything needs time to germinate. We must learn to accept this. When we are fully ready to accept our good, it will manifest itself. About a year later I saw Rod at a party and knew he looked very familiar but couldn't quite place him. I finally approached him and said, "I know you from somewhere. I'm Jeri Land." He said, "Oh yes, you are Judy's sister. I'm Rod." Later that evening he found me and my date in another room. He came up and began talking with us.

My date was going through a divorce and was quite bitter that his wife seemed to be so happy in a new relationship. I thought Rod was wonderful the way he supported my date. He said things like, "The way for you to have what you want in your life is to support her having what she wants." I thought he was brilliant and had been sent to me by God himself. Rod could of course feel my energy and continued to support and encourage my date with his kind words even though my date obviously didn't want to hear them. He didn't want the support but didn't know how to stop the process. My date didn't want to hear what Rod was saying. He wanted Rod and me to agree with him that his ex-wife should not be happy in her new relationship. We weren't buying it. The fact is, being generous and wishing others well opens you up to your good. We really cannot have for ourselves that which we want to prevent others from having. So in this case, my date did not want his ex-wife to be happy in another relationship, so how was he going to find a fulfilling and satisfying relationship for himself? **He was actually blocking his own happiness by wishing her unhappiness.** I hope this makes sense to you because it is a very important point.

Truth be told, Rod was really supporting my date for my benefit. It was his way of letting me know what he was about. I knew that night Rod was the one for me. I thought,

"He is my soul mate." I gave him my card before we left the party and said, "Call me." He did and we began our journey together. He brought Dan, Kym, and Tyler to me and we had our son Wes between us. We filled our home with love.

Learn the act of allowing what you want into your life. Allow great relationships. Allow more money into your life. Allow yourself to find a career that you love. All you need to do is to simply identify what you want, get into the feeling place of having it, take appropriate action on what shows up and then allow it to flow to you by holding your focus there. When you understand these laws and put them to use consciously and deliberately, you put yourself in a place of non-resistance. How do you know if you are really willing and allowing? By noticing how you feel, your emotions are always your guide. Whenever you are in a place of harmony, you are in a place of allowing or willingness. When you are in this place of harmony and willingness, all things are possible. Take the time to get very clear about what you wish to create in your life and then look inside to see if you are really _willing_ to have it happen, if you are really _willing to allow it in now._

CHAPTER 6
— CHANGING YOUR PATTERNS —

Without inspiration, the best powers of the mind remain dormant; there is a fuel in us which needs to be ignited with sparks.

–Johann Gottfried Von Herder

6
CHAPTER

I met a sweet young man when I was 18 years old who I thought was the most handsome man I had ever seen. We met and fell in love. At 20, he and I decided to wed and sought out a church where we would enjoy exchanging vows. We discovered the Church of Religious Science (currently known as The Center for Spiritual Living), which we both loved. While my young marriage didn't last, my involvement in the church and the study of Metaphysics did.

> SEE YOURSELF MORE IN THE LIGHT OF YOU BEING PERFECT, WHOLE AND COMPLETE, EVEN WITH YOUR PERCEIVED IMPERFECTIONS.

My belief in myself blossomed as I studied foundational concepts found in Metaphysics. The basic tenet of Metaphysics is the knowledge that, "to think is to create". While I explored the concept that whatever the mind can conceive and believe it will achieve, I didn't have any credible evidence yet to support it other than those who seemed to get it without question. I decided if it was good enough for them that it would be okay for me to borrow someone else's faith. I encourage you too to feel free to borrow my faith and explore Metaphysical principles.

So my transformation began. Every day I wrote prayers acknowledging who I was in truth and began to appreciate myself at a whole other level, the level that *I imagined God saw in me*. In effect, I started shedding my old internal beliefs about my imperfections and transformed those limiting thoughts to seeing myself more in the light of me being perfect, whole and complete, even with my perceived imperfections.

I discovered and acknowledged that I was one with the Universe, One with the One Mind and that the Infinite Intelligence works through me. In those days I never used the word God because it conjured up, from inherited beliefs, a visual of a Man with a beard on a throne. This visual created a feeling of separation from God as though he was there and I was here. I no longer have this image of God. I do see what was revealed to me, when in boarding school, that God is in me, all around me, through me and is present everywhere including what we call the physical. I discovered that when I was clear in my acknowledgement of these truths, and would state what I wanted to accomplish in my life, little demonstrations started to appear as proof that I was creating my reality.

My confidence began to build and I took on more and more. What I discovered was that this wonderful lesson never ends and is as fresh with me today as it was back then. In your life, as you choose to be in a state of growth you will find yourself taking on more and more resulting in creating a more abundant life for you and those around you. Inside all of us there is the knowing that we can be more, do more and contribute more; so let's encourage each other to let it flow forth.

Of all our needs in life the only two that bring us true fulfillment are growth and contribution. Contribution can look many different ways. As we grow we contribute more in our space just by our "beingness". As we grow we show others the way. As we prosper we can contribute financially to causes that are meaningful to us. And we can inspire others and take the hand of others and show them the way. This has become my mission and purpose in life. We all have had hard times in life; these are our gifts. These are our opportunities for growth and our opportunities to measure our growth.

FIND YOUR TRUTH

I took my life on and explored various jobs that the Universe put in front of me. I started with ballroom dancing where I wore high heels eight hours a day, learned all the steps from both the female and male perspective and taught men how to dance and to lead their partners. It was fun and also challenging. It was during this time that I got married and teaching ballroom dancing at night was not congruent with a happy marriage. So, I entered Beauty College only to discover that, while I loved doing hair, I did not want to be in the hair styling business. I then explored different sales jobs where I got my knees skinned and nose bloodied. One day I took a job at a drapery manufacturing company where I earned minimum wage. What I remember most about that job was that I came home with knots on top of knots in my back and shoulders because I was out of integrity with myself and felt powerless there. For example, when someone would call in to speak with my boss, I would politely ask their name and ask them to hold while I got him to the phone. My boss would then say, "Tell him I am not in." I thought, "He doesn't pay me enough to lie." Actually, no one could pay me enough to lie for them so I knew I had to leave.

I had to find something in more alignment with my true path and purpose. Frustrated, I then made a list of questions calling upon the Universe for answers. How did I want to see myself in a job or business? What was I wearing? How did I speak? How did others see me? Did I make a difference in the world? Did what I do have value in the economy? Fortunately, my Mother had often told me I should get into real estate and, given my then state of mind, I always said I would never do that. As I wrote my list of things that were important to me regarding liberty and how I saw myself in the world, real estate kept coming up as a possible path to all the things that now seemed important to me. I made a decision to go to real estate school with the condition that I would not actually commit to getting into the business. Given my initial resistance, I believed that I would not be successful at it. So I took it a step at a time. I committed to finishing the school and getting my license. As it turned out I loved the school and did go into the business.

GOD IS IN YOU, ALL AROUND YOU, THROUGH YOU AND IS PRESENT EVERYWHERE INCLUDING WHAT WE CALL THE PHYSICAL.

I actually made more money in the first 3 months than I had ever made in a year before. Amazingly, this was in 1974 when the real estate market was one of the worst in history. I made the decision to not listen to the naysayers and I

> AS YOU CHOOSE TO BE IN A STATE OF GROWTH YOU WILL FIND YOURSELF TAKING ON MORE AND MORE RESULTING IN CREATING A MORE ABUNDANT LIFE FOR YOU AND THOSE AROUND YOU.

committed fully to the business, a successful decision that lasted for the next 14 years in which I sold literally thousands of homes.

HIDDEN ADDICTIONS

Along the way, as I searched for the love of my life, I found myself in the position of coaching the men in my life on how they could be successful. I always seemed to see them bigger than they saw themselves. Meanwhile, I failed to focus on seeing my own great potential. My first husband was a very nice man with no drive or ambition. I had big dreams for him but he did not share my dreams. One day he said, "I just want to 'boogaloo' through life with a piece of straw in my mouth." I was quite clear at that point in our relationship that we were not meant to be for very long. He had every right to desire that kind of life but I knew it was not for me. I wanted more, much more.

I moved on in and out of a few relationships and then met the man who cured me. While this was a stormy, unsettling and unrewarding relationship, I learned so much from it. I cannot emphasize enough how this was a pivotal watershed in my life. Please pay close attention here, for this chapter in my life, while pivotal for me, will hopefully be more meaningful for you in helping you to discover your underlying attraction and investment in relationships that don't necessarily serve you.

What I didn't understand, at the time, was that I was attracted to this man because his energy was familiar. It was familiar in that I experienced pain and uncertainty including a fear that he might walk away at any time. For reasons that I didn't understand at that time, this feeling of uncertainty was both appealing and attractive. He and his friends drove cars that appeared to me a symbol of success. These friends were very similar in their personalities and this group had a leader who was very condescending to women including me. It amazes me today how I ignored all the signals because of my interest in this guy. Since he seemed to have a desire to be successful and I had a desire to support him in becoming more than he saw for himself, I saw promise in the relationship and began my coaching techniques with him.

He ultimately pulled away from his friends and appeared to be taking his life on. My financial coaching appeared to be working. I saw what looked like significant progress and then things would just fall apart. Finally, I said to him that it was time for us to have a heart-to-heart talk and get to the bottom of what was blocking him. I asked many questions to draw him out, questions to invoke his introspection so that he could discover for himself what the block was inside himself. After much discussion he finally uttered the words that were pivotal to me. He said, "I think what it is for me is, if I am successful, you will get what you want." I

INSIDE ALL OF US THERE IS THE KNOWING THAT WE CAN BE MORE, DO MORE AND CONTRIBUTE MORE; SO LET'S ENCOURAGE EACH OTHER TO LET IT FLOW FORTH.

knew at that moment and pointed out to him the fact that he was willing to sabotage his own success and happiness to keep me from getting what he perceived I wanted for me.

I sincerely hoped that this would be a breakthrough for him that would help to launch him into a life of alignment with himself and to see how this has gotten in his way of other relationships and would always be a block for him until he turned it around. I was excited that he sourced his truth and now it was up to him to choose a different way to operate, or not.

For me, it was so revealing and so freeing. I knew that first of all I was wasting my time in a relationship with a person who was so committed to me not having what I want in my life that he was willing to sabotage his own happiness and success to make certain of it. It was also freeing because for the first time in my life I looked to myself to see what was really there. I began to see, for the very first time, that I not only had ambition, I also had moxie. I clearly was able to coach others, as long as they wanted it, and I seemed to have a sixth sense about just what to say to motivate that individual to move forward in his or her life and to discover for themselves what was going on inside them.

So, I thought, why not me? After much thought and soul-searching I decided to take myself on. I thought, I will coach me like I am another person. For the first time I had someone who genuinely wanted to break through her money barrier, was willing to listen and do as told and had the same desires as I. That someone, of course, was none other than _me_. So he cured me from putting all my attention on someone who didn't want it and I put my attention on someone who did, that being me.

You may wonder, as have I, what drew me to this man in the first place. Through this process of writing this book it has become painfully clear to me that one of the big attractions was the familiarity of pain and uncertainty. I was in a relationship with him for two years before I meekly uttered the words that I thought he might have a drinking problem. Once I realized this and was able to fully acknowledge that he was an alcoholic, I then realized that my ex-husband had a drinking problem and my own mother did as well. I began learning what I could about this issue in people's lives and quickly realized that I had a need to be with a person who was attached to alcohol. I was sharp enough to understand that jumping right out of that relationship would do me no good for I would just go out and get another one just like him. I realized that I had to work through my own needs that drew me into this kind of unsettling and disruptive relationship.

> AS WE PROSPER WE CAN CONTRIBUTE FINANCIALLY TO CAUSES THAT ARE MEANINGFUL TO US.

My discoveries continued whereby my glimpses became clearer and clearer that it was familiar to me due to how I held my childhood experiences. I held them as painful, fearful, and I felt powerless. These patterns of uncertainty were centered on my mother and father divorcing when I was eight and then being sent to boarding school; I never had a vote. They decided the direction my life would take. And the worst experience of all was my Daddy crashing his plane and leaving me when I was twelve. I then lived with my mother until I was 18 and watched her struggle with alcohol. Since this pain was familiar, in a strange way it is what I expected, looked for and attracted me to a relationship. Once I became aware of this pattern in my life and what I was attracted to in relationship, I knew that if I was ever going to have what I wanted in my life, I needed to face and work through these issues, <u>find happiness within and learn to become attracted to something *unfamiliar* to me now.</u>

Take an honest look at your life now. What have you attracted into your life? Whatever is there is what you have attracted to you. If you desire something different, you have to become attracted to the unfamiliar.

I had to see myself as if I were another person in order to be more objective. In order for me to coach myself I had to engage the true "I" that is different from the ego. I became consciously aware of my connection to the Infinite Intelligence and allowed it to work through me as I worked with the ego called Jeri. So I began my work in earnest, coaching me. This was rigorous, daily meditations clearing through all the old cobwebs of beliefs about myself and women in business. I had already decided I didn't have what it takes and then when I decided that I might, I was afraid to become what I thought that would be.

I had made decisions about women in business. I thought women who were successful were hard and unfeminine. I certainly did not want to be that. I discovered that if you disdain something, as fast as you move toward it, it will move away from you at the same speed. It became clear that past attempts at being successful were sabotaged by me because fundamentally I saw a successful woman as hard and unfeminine and I did not want to be that. I realized that I had to change my thinking about myself and women in the business world if I was ever to have what I wanted. So you see, going out and working hard is only a very small part of it.

If you don't deal with the underlying beliefs about yourself, you might as well stay home. I had to consciously choose to change the beliefs that I had adopted when I was growing up to this point in my life. So I did. I started the process everyday of declaring who I was in reality, not my old beliefs. I had to consciously choose to see myself in a very different way. I chose every day to see myself successful, dressed well and providing a valuable service to others. Then I had an opportunity to work, without compensation, for a woman in my industry who was very successful. I jumped at the chance to spend my weekends in her office so that I could see what she was doing that worked so well for her.

One of the greatest lessons I learned working there was, not only was she a very competent and capable businessperson, she was a lady through and through. She had a different style than I, and I could see that I would have my own style as I moved along in my profession but I never had to give up my femininity; in fact it would only enhance me as a businessperson. This was the most joyful lesson I learned. This removed such a big block for me. I think this one thing was much bigger than I knew. I think I only really recognized it when she wiped it away with her lovely style. Thank you, Victoria, wherever you are today.

CONSCIOUSLY CHOOSE TO SEE YOURSELF IN A VERY DIFFERENT WAY.

So every day I would remind myself who I was in reality, one who is capable of anything I desire, and see myself as a feminine successful businesswoman. I would see the kind of money that I wanted to earn and held it with ease as if it were already mine. I just got clear about the money and didn't worry about it. I just focused on my personal growth in the business. I dug in hard to be as good as I could be to prove to others and myself that I was truly valuable and an asset to anyone blessed enough to do business with me. If this sounds egotistical to you, I encourage you to look deeply inside yourself and ask why. **It is essential that you hold yourself in the highest regard if you are truly going to offer a good service to others.** If I didn't provide a superlative service to others, they should not do business with me. This goes for you too. If you are not willing to be all you can be and offer the best service possible, people should do business with one who is. They should find someone who is willing to be all they can be. I was willing and hungry to be all I could be.

Beliefs are basically concepts that we either make up on our own or that we take over from someone else. Belief is a built-in function of your consciousness and is a commanding tool that shapes your reality. It is so powerful that, when adaptively formulated from many people, it can shift mass consciousness and lead to profound changes in our society. It even has the power to shift the collective consciousness of the entire civilization. St. Augustine, in the 5th century said, "Unless you believe, you will not understand."

By the act of believing, we form a unique structure in our consciousness as an energy pattern that acts like a blueprint for what we will experience in our life. You have a choice of what to do – you always have a choice. You can simply react to the situation and let your mind tell you what to do, by calling on one of the old thoughts that automatically came up to guide you <u>or you can deliberately make a choice to create a new thought that supports you moving in the direction of your dreams, ambition and desires.</u>

CHOOSE EVERYDAY TO SEE YOURSELF SUCCESSFUL, DRESSED WELL AND PROVIDING A VALUABLE SERVICE TO OTHERS.

A reaction is an unconscious response to a situation; most of the time it is a reflection of a past belief. It is a choice-less and powerless approach to handling a situation. An action, however, is a deliberate choice you make. It is a response to a situation that is based on the result of consciously analyzing and contemplating the situation. It empowers you and moves your life further along the path you have chosen. Beliefs are very powerful in determining whether you react or act. One way to determine what beliefs you want to take on is simply by looking for what the reality would be and what a particular belief would create. Is this belief supporting what you want to experience or not?

MANIFESTING BELIEFS

One very important phrase that has slipped into current thought is "to manifest". In plain English it simply means to create or cause whatever you are dreaming of to become real.

All good that is to be manifested in our lives is already an accomplished fact in the Infinite Power and is released through our recognition or spoken word. Because of this, you have to be extraordinarily careful to speak your words correctly. Become more aware of how you use side comments, jokes, etc., all under the guise that you are just being funny. Notice how these words may be a covert way to communicate some hidden belief or judgment about another person or yourself. Become more aware of how you speak about yourself and how you speak to yourself, your "self-talk". The fact is that the results we create in our lives are a direct reflection of our current belief systems. The good news is we have the ability to alter our beliefs to those that serve us now with choices that we make each day of the thoughts and words that we think and speak.

I recommend that in the morning you start your day with the spoken word. Speak well to yourself as you stand in front of the mirror in the naturalness of your body, exactly as it is in its current shape and form. Find its beauty and embrace with love, not judgment, any thoughts of what you would like to change.

It is important to comprehend how the subconscious mind, with its collected and inherited beliefs, controls so much of what you think is possible in your life. Since we are bound by the limited expectancies of the subconscious, we must enlarge our expectancies in order to receive in a larger way. This requires being willing to enter into new and unchartered waters and welcoming any fear, rather than resisting it. A question you may ask yourself is, "What do I really want?" While becoming clear about what you want is an essential part of a process to being and having more, it is important to become aware of the role of your subconscious beliefs in affecting the outcome. <u>Without realizing it, you often limit your thinking about what you want by what your beliefs, embedded in your subconscious mind, tell you about your capability to produce.</u> <u>This belief then shapes what you say you want, which in turn gets you no further than you are today.</u>

Let's imagine that you want a better paying job. Immediately and without hesitation, the subconscious mind may start reminding you about the fact that you never finished college and therefore would not be able to get the better paying job, especially if in your conscious mind you create a thought that a degree would be required. This is another example of your mind arguing for your limitations. Why does your mind do that? Your mind is a wonderful gift whose purpose is to keep you alive and safe. When you were a child and you put your hand near something hot, it instinctively had you pull away from it. It always is turned on and is always ready to keep you safe. So here you come asking for a better job and the old beliefs don't like change so they remind you of things, like the fact that you didn't finish college, to keep you in the familiar.

YOU NEED TO HOLD YOURSELF IN THE HIGHEST REGARD IF YOU ARE TRULY GOING TO OFFER A GOOD SERVICE TO OTHERS.

On top of that, you may have a belief that fear is not good or healthy, when in actuality, your fear can be this wonderful gift that validates that you are growing and on a new and exciting path. Obviously, we are not talking about life-threatening fear here but rather the fear that shows up when we step out from what is familiar. As we step out of that familiar space, we can either call it fear or we can learn to rename it as excitement and growth so that we can hold what is going on differently. So the next time you experience fear, welcome it with open arms and try renaming it and see how that feels. A man I met named Edrick Dunand who does corporate coaching, using sports cars as a metaphor, says that when you feel your body start to shake, it means that the chemicals in your body are getting you ready for "peak performance". I love that way of looking at it. Remember, unless you're willing to offer your wants and desires to the Universe, they won't manifest as reality. You need to let the Universe know that you are ready and willing.

BY THE ACT OF BELIEVING WE FORM A UNIQUE STRUCTURE IN OUR CONSCIOUSNESS AS AN ENERGY PATTERN THAT ACTS LIKE A BLUEPRINT FOR WHAT WE WILL EXPERIENCE IN OUR LIFE.

By continually affirming your thoughts and desires, they become a belief rooted in the subconscious. As a young child, we did this instinctively and probably without much conscious thought. As we get older, we must make the conscious effort to affirm our thoughts and desires in order to impress them into the subconscious as a belief. **An effective way to prepare your mind to embrace a new belief is to start with gratitude.** By acknowledging the blessings that life has bestowed, you open the pores to your subconscious mind to being available to all that the Universe has in store for you. <u>What if you discovered that the Universe responds exactly to the level of your willingness and openness to have what you want?</u> You'd probably be more willing to let go of the limiting beliefs under which you operate and express in reality.

Imagine then if you were to express gratitude for your divine right to choose your thoughts. What do you imagine the results in your life would look like then? Give thanks repeatedly for what you have received and are about to receive. This is easy enough to state in the abstract, but a little more difficult when confronted with a problem. <u>When we release the attachment to our problems, we'll have instantaneous manifestation. Releasing means that you focus on the solution to the problem and not the problem.</u> Too often when confronted with a problem, we are drawn into the drama surrounding it. We even reinforce the drama by finding others to commiserate with us. This is the time to focus and see only the solution, even if the solution is not clearly evident.

Let go of having to create the solution, put it in the hands of the Universe and continue to be open and respond to whatever the Universe puts before you. If, for example, you have doubts about whether a solution will manifest, immediately counteract that doubt with an affirmation such as: "*I give thanks for the knowing that I am one with the Infinite Intelligence and Power. That Power works through me now and always; I am grateful for this knowing. I remain clear that which I desire (be specific) already exists in the Universe and is manifested in my life now; for this I am grateful".*

Remember, when I speak of manifesting, I mean what we are creating in our life. If it is a relationship you are manifesting, you must allow for the individual's free will. Do not attempt to manifest a specific person into your life but rather the essence of the person, qualities and traits you desire in your relationship. Remember, there is no time or space in the Superconscious; therefore our words instantly reach their destination.

> OUR GREATEST GIFTS OFTEN COME TO US THROUGH OUR GREATEST CHALLENGES.

You can train your mind to receive flashes of inspiration. The Infinite Intelligence transcends the limitation of the conscious mind, and is always the center of life, containing health, wealth, love and perfect self-expression. As you are what you think, if you think positively you'll feel positively. Likewise, if you think you have certain qualities and talents, that's how you'll be. Even if you don't have these characteristics now, if you think you have them, you'll develop them and your self-esteem will soar.

There is much said about "thinking positively" that I believe is misunderstood. I'm not talking about running around with a fake smile on your face and pretending that things are all good when you are in the face of despair. What I am talking about is the ability to seek and find the gifts in every situation and circumstance.

When my Daddy, who was the love of my life, died, it took me way too many years to see not only the gift that I had him as my Daddy and I was able to have him in my life for twelve years of life, but also that he left me to grow and learn and become the grounded and strong individual who I am. I may not have developed into this strength had he lived. Certainly I would be different than I am. Not good or bad, just that my gifts were in his passing as well as in his life.

ALL GOOD THAT IS TO BE MANIFESTED IN OUR LIVES IS ALREADY AN ACCOMPLISHED FACT IN THE INFINITE POWER AND IS RELEASED THROUGH OUR RECOGNITION OR SPOKEN WORD.

I feel fairly certain that my ability for compassion and empathy of others is due to my own life's path. So when I say think positively, I am really saying to seek and find the gifts in any situation and circumstance in your life. Our challenges are our greatest gifts. It is through these challenges that we grow if we choose to do so. It is always up to you to choose. The sooner we learn to embrace our challenges as our gifts, the sooner we find peace and joy in our hearts.

There is one more story I wish to share with you before I close this chapter. It is a story of a friend of mine who in the deepest moment of despair, actually facing a life-and-death situation, reached deep inside herself for her strength and determination. Some would say what finally happened was a miracle and I would agree; however, it was more than that, for it was a moment of complete commitment and determination; it was a definitive decision. Please read Jan's story and you will know what I mean.

"The power of an instantaneous decision saved my life, literally. Several years ago, I served on the Board of Directors at our zoo. During the largest fundraising event for the year, I was mauled by one of the tigers that escaped. The tiger knocked me down, and I knew that at that moment, I was fine and they would get him back in the cage. To my left and inches from me, I noticed the enormous paw of the 600 pound cat, and again, I knew that I was fine at that moment, and they would get him back in the cage, and then I realized that I could feel his chest touching my back. Again, the same thought went through my mind, knowing I was fine and that they would get him back in the cage. I heard an awful sound as the tiger bit into my head, and then I saw the blood pouring down on the ground under my face. My next thought was, "Am I going to survive?" "YES" came immediately, followed by, "No one else is going to raise my son." Recently I put it together that the power of that decision did save me. There was a policeman very nearby who shot at the tiger, missed him and hit me. That shot did scare the tiger off me, but left me with such a wound to my leg that doctors later told me it was a miracle that I was able to walk again. Was it a miracle? Perhaps; it was a decision most definitely.

–Jan Gold

So Jan tells the story from such a bottom line and responsible place that it may be difficult for you to comprehend the enormous power of her strength and determination. Literally a tiger escaped from its cage; actually two tigers escaped. Jan was taking people on a tour and one of the tigers jumped on her and took her down. The people surrounding her were in a panic, running around trying to figure out what to do about two wild tigers out of their cage and one of them mauling this woman. Not the kind of scene you plan for as you wake in the morning. Jan knew she was being attacked but she never focused on the problem; she held her mind firm to the solution. This is a lesson for us all in every situation in life. No matter what challenges we face, we must hold our thoughts on the solution only. Never give in to the thoughts of the problem. Had she allowed herself to think about what was happening to her at that moment, she would likely have panicked and no telling how she might have riled the tiger even more. As it was, she remained calm and focused on the solution. *"They will get the tiger back in his cage and I am fine."* When she heard the sound of him biting into her skull and saw the blood pouring down onto the ground beneath her, she became more determined. *"No one else will raise my son."* Those are powerful words from a determined mother to save her own life for the love of her son.

If only we were all that determined each day to create a better life for ourselves, for the love and appreciation of our life here on this earth, or perhaps for the sense of responsibility to make a difference in the life of another.

I just wanted to share this story with you because even though most of us have never faced the actual living tiger in our lives, we have often felt that some of the challenges we have faced were nearly that scary. Notice in your life when you focus on the scary problem, you create more of the scary problem. The way out is to focus on the solution. As you focus on the solution, the scary goes away.

I hope this helps. I was so moved by Jan's story that I really wanted to share it with you. She is an inspiration in so many ways. Her story is such a great metaphor for the challenges we all face. In her case it was really a tiger.

CHAPTER 7
— MAKING SENSE OF THE ONENESS —

Learn to become still and to take your attention away from what you don't want, and all the emotional charge around it, and place your attention on what you wish to experience.

–Michael Beckwith

7
CHAPTER

Most of us have grown up in a belief that we live in a disconnected Universe. From the moment we are born there is a persistent pattern of the illusion of separation formed by the very labels we use to identify ourselves. The first is being labeled as boy or girl, followed with an individualized first name and our group family name. It continues as we become identified by our race and nationality, our religion, our group of friends and our school. We compete in sports as one team against another team and no wonder we are well on our way to assuming we live in a disconnected Universe.

The cost of this inherited view is that you may see the world in an "us and them" mindset which in turn limits your ability to live an open and inclusive life conducive to your personal growth. So what happens when you depart from this view of separateness and begin to explore and accept that there is a Oneness and that we are all connected? So what happens when you become bold enough to explore the concept further and consider that everyone and everything is connected? When you accept that there is only Oneness, you experience a very different reality with more rewarding results. Life becomes this energetic adventure where you create and attract the best in yourself and others, especially when facing your challenges head-on. You begin to notice and experience that the thoughts you choose actually do manifest the results in your life and with that knowing you realize the benefits of this knowledge and its acceptance as truth. You realize the ineffectiveness of blaming others and you experience the euphoric realization that *I am completely responsible for my life and all that is in it.*

> WHEN YOU ACCEPT THAT THERE IS ONLY ONENESS, YOU EXPERIENCE A VERY DIFFERENT REALITY WITH MORE REWARDING RESULTS.

Any struggle you may have with this concept of Oneness is usually rooted in your inherited familial conditioning reinforced by your religious beliefs, beliefs that you typically had poured into you in childhood, without your vote. Yet, somehow in moments when you least expect it, you experience this Oneness. It might appear as a flash of inspiration. Suddenly you feel this motivation inside to get something done that is meaningful to you, something so strong and true that nothing gets in your way. Have you ever wondered why you were so inspired and motivated? Simply stated, you are connected as one with the Infinite Intelligence and when you put aside your limited thinking, your power and presence as an expression of this Infinite Intelligence takes hold. Rumi, a 13th century Persian mystic and poet, may well have spoken it best when he wrote that, **"The whole Universe exists within you, so ask all from yourself."**

THE OVERVIEW EFFECT

For those of us who want something more current than the 13th century, you need to look no further for some evidence of our Oneness than to our astronauts who have come back to earth with a different consciousness than when they left. The belief that we are one with the Universe is referred to by some as the "Overview Effect" which first became noteworthy with accounts shared by returning space astronauts in the late sixties. The acute awareness of all matter as synergistically connected, described by these astronauts, is similar to religious experiences described by Buddhist monks.

YOU ARE COMPLETELY RESPONSIBLE FOR YOUR LIFE AND ALL THAT IS IN IT.

On March 6, 1969, during his spacewalk outside his Apollo 9 vehicle, Rusty Schweickart experienced a feeling that the whole Universe was profoundly connected. In his own words, he said: "When you go around the earth in an hour and a half, you begin to recognize that your identity is with that whole thing. That makes a change . . it comes through to you so powerfully that you're the sensing element for Man." Again in 1971, Edgar Mitchell, an Apollo 14 astronaut, experienced this sense of universal connectedness. He describes an instantaneous feeling of bliss, timelessness, and connectedness engulfing him. In Mitchell's heightened state of awareness, he experienced that each atom of his cells was connected to the entire Universe just outside his capsule window. After decades of study and contemplation about his experience, he believes that the feeling of "Oneness" with the Universe is a consequence of the little understood Quantum Physics whose study leads you to the conclusion that everyone and everything is connected as energy and vibrating at the sub-atomic level.

Where does this feeling of Oneness come from and why? Their experiences, along with several similar accounts by other astronauts, captivated the attention of scientists who study the brain. Andy Newberg, a neuroscientist/physician who specialized in located neurological markers of brains in states of altered consciousness, believes there is a definite difference in a person who has traveled through space. He has actually pinpointed specific regions of the brains of transcendental meditators and devout nuns that correlate to this sense of connectedness. Andy Newberg authored a fascinating book called *"How God Changes Your Mind"* dealing with this topic in depth.

Good stuff; however, if you are struggling with getting this concept or you are someone who may want to get it but thinks that it will take a lot of hard work and study, you may find comfort in the words of Deepak Chopra: *"Awareness isn't something you achieve, it's what happens when you stop trying so hard."* Many of us have heard the words, "We are made in the image and likeness of God". In essence, Jesus said in John 14:12 that, "All these things I do, you can do and more." What does all this mean? Assume for the moment, that what it means is that you are infinitely connected and one with the Infinite Intelligence or Oneness.

In such a Truth, you would have the opportunity to participate in the creation, attraction and manifestation of every result in your life. You would see others, including your perceived enemies and people with whom you do not resonate, conjoined in the very Oneness; and you would love and support them in a dignified, respectful manner. You would see them at their higher self striving to be closer to their Truth and support them in being so. You would pray for them in a holistic manner. Tibetan Buddhist leader His Holiness the Seventeenth Gyalwang Karmapa describes how Oneness is experienced. First, he says, as a breadth of vision cultivated through meditation and contemplation, and second as the harmony arising from mutual support and self-sacrifice of the individual and society. Close your eyes and create a vision of the world as if you were fully aware and experiencing your connection to your Oneness. What would you change? What would you teach?

I'M RIGHT

So why don't we do this all the time? Our minds have been conditioned since birth in a right/wrong, us/them perceived reality where it is easier to make someone wrong than acknowledge them to be right. As an adult, there was a moment in my relationship with my sister when we had not been getting along. This went on for some time. We had mostly reconciled our differences but I kept a certain distance not feeling that I could fully trust her. We were about to take a trip together and I shared with a friend, who was also a personal coach, my concern of being away from home with my sister because I was afraid we might get into an argument and I would be stuck in this isolated area with no easy way home.

My friend Jean, and I should say in capital letters, FRIEND, said to me, "Jeri, you may not want to hear this but you are more interested in being right than you are in your relationship with your sister." I was completely floored by this comment and wanted more than anything to explain to her the error of her comment but I realized that everything I was about to say would only validate what she had just said to me. Here I was, a person who was keenly aware of our Oneness and clearly understood what that meant, yet with my own sister, who I love dearly, I was willing to hang out in righteousness rather than come from love and appreciation for my sister. When I took some time alone to contemplate this shocking reality about myself, I realized that I had been willing to sacrifice a relationship that could never be replaced for my ego and need to be right. I further realized that if I lost my sister, I would die a thousand deaths inside yet I had been throwing our relationship away. I certainly did not feel "right" at that moment. I felt stupid, petty, and small. I knew that I could make a difference in our relationship and I was determined to do just that.

YOU ARE CONNECTED AS ONE WITH THE INFINITE INTELLIGENCE AND WHEN YOU PUT ASIDE YOUR LIMITED THINKING, YOUR POWER AND PRESENCE AS AN EXPRESSION OF THIS INFINITE INTELLIGENCE TAKES HOLD.

My sister and I did go on that trip and we had a wonderful time together and we talked about how we had both been behaving with each other and vowed never to let anything come between us again. We realized that when we were out of sorts with each other that there was a part of us that was always unhappy, no matter what else we were doing. Love is a powerful thing and it can heal all things. Judy and I now have a little trigger between us that we can call upon whenever we are starting to feel scared. First of all there is the understanding and agreement between us that we both want a loving and safe relationship so I carry a little red foam nose in my purse. When Judy and I are together and I think she is getting testy with me, I just pull out the red nose and she cracks up. All I really have to do is threaten to pull out the nose and she cracks up. That pretty much ends all arguments between us.

We have had a couple of bumps in the road since that day but they are minor and they do not last. We both know how important our relationship is with each other and we protect and defend it fiercely now. All relationships can be that deep and wonderful when we are willing to give up our need to be right and just love and appreciate the other person for who they are in their truth. We don't always have to like how they show up any more than we would not always like the way we show up, but we can still see them in their higher self. The same goes for ourselves. Love and forgive yourself; love and forgive others.

YOU HAVE THE OPPORTUNITY TO PARTICIPATE IN THE CREATION, ATTRACTION AND MANIFESTATION OF EVERY RESULT IN YOUR LIFE.

Knowing the Truth is both a phenomenal gift as well as an awesome responsibility and maybe that is why many choose to hide behind the familiar, inherited beliefs that keep us separated from one another. In fact, I have experienced being with individuals who are more interested in sharing negativity and righteousness about someone who they may have perceived did them some harm rather than solely speaking about their individual responsibility in the matter. Jerry Seinfeld was once asked why he never uses the "F" word in his comedy. He said that, "if you have to use the 'F' word, you've run out of material". In the same way, when we find ourselves blindly following our almost natural inclination in being "right" and its natural progression into its close cousin, "victimhood", we too have run out of our high vibration spiritual material.

At the birth of our soul, we are given the connection to this wonderful Oneness. Our basic state of consciousness is formed by our our parent's level of consciousness and early life experiences. For many of us, we abandoned the very materials of Oneness that will bring us such fulfillment, love and joy in our lives. The great news is that you haven't run out of material. You have an infinite supply and you will find it inside, and not without, as Rumi pointed out 8 centuries ago. *"God has not given up on you, so why would you?"* Deepak Chopra was interviewed on the subject of Oneness and he shared that there is an old phrase in India which states that *every child born is proof that God has not given up on humanity.*

I'M CONFUSED

As you allow yourself to consider that all is connected, a paradox to your conditioned thinking may arise. The paradox is that you intuitively know that you are an individual expression, you're "I am", and you don't appear to be Mary, Renee or Mike. How can there be Oneness in this apparent dual reality which may seem in conflict with a concept of a singular, connected Universe? The answer may be found in acceptance that the Universe is one with many different forms or expressions and manifestations. Remember the Aspen grove of trees; while each tree is unique, if you look underground you will discover that what appears to be many trees is actually one connected tree with many expressions. In scientific study, it would be that atoms cluster into a form yet never change their basic fundamental elements. Just like the cluster of water can appear in the form of water, ice, snow, or vapor – all look different – the Oneness can manifest itself in different forms too.

In Bruce Lipton's book, *"Biology of Belief"*, he explains that each of us is a cluster of cells and on a more expansive view that we, as a group, are an attracted cluster of cells connected and vibrating in the Oneness. You are simply combining your energy with the Universe. As you do this, the Universe continues to expand, like adding fuel to the flame; the more fuel you add, the larger the flame becomes. The more our energy unites with the Universe, the stronger the Collective Consciousness becomes. You become a part of that energy, to where your Infinite Intelligence reaches out to others and in turn is contributed back to you. Deepak Chopra and others refer to the idea of "critical mass". We all have the opportunity to contribute to the new universal consciousness. As we contribute of ourselves with love and acceptance, we are helping this planet reach critical mass of a new consciousness of love, joy, and acceptance in the world.

WATCH YOUR THOUGHTS

So many of us worry incessantly about what is going on in our lives and how we think we are supposed to be or what we think we are supposed to have. Perhaps you worry about what others think of you. It is said that "worry" is a prayer for what we don't want. If it is true that the subconscious mind listens to all your thoughts, then it might be very important to pay close attention to what you spend your time thinking about. When you stay clear and focused on what you want and you fill your thoughts and emotions with your good, this is what you will create in your life. Fill your thoughts with family, love, balance, prosperity, and abundance and this is what you will create. The service you render to others, out of true love and affection, all aid to increase your spiritual character, which in turn helps you to become aware of your Oneness with the Infinite Intelligence. The Universal Laws have nothing to do with our human laws. The Universal Laws are eternal and remain constant, whereas our human laws are ever-changing.

OUR MINDS HAVE BEEN CONDITIONED SINCE BIRTH IN A RIGHT/WRONG, US/THEM PERCEIVED REALITY WHERE IT IS EASIER TO MAKE SOMEONE WRONG THAN ACKNOWLEDGE THEM TO BE RIGHT.

THE ULTIMATE CONNECTION

When you tap into the Superconscious, you're functioning on a higher vibrational level. Many of us find this level through meditation and prayer whereby you set aside disconnected concepts and surrender to the experience of connection to all and all that is possible. It is as though your brain disappears and your thoughts literally move through you in a fluid connection to something you sense as God. Nothing is misunderstood.

You deliver the exact intended message as it was meant to be. Since you are co-creator with the Universe, you are connected through your collective thoughts which enable you to ultimately own every major event that comes into your life. Such events teach the most powerful and life-changing lessons to us.

All major life events that happen are basically programmed into your blueprints by you to further your spiritual development. These blueprints are placed in your subconscious mind to help you fulfill your individual pattern of growth. Universal growth knows no limits; it can teach one individual or it can teach many; pretty hefty stuff. Wayne Dyer tells a story of a moment with his daughter. They were having a disagreement and she was upset with him. He pointed out that we choose everything in life including her choosing him as her father which silenced her for a moment. After thinking for a moment she replied by saying, "Well, I must have been in a hurry."

Make no mistake about it, Wayne absolutely meant what he said. The majority of people seem to find it hard to take personal accountability to that level; how about you? Your soul knows best what lessons you need to attract to you, even if consciously you are unaware of that. If you find it difficult to accept that you are responsible for it all, then, *at a minimum, accept that you choose your experience of those events. If you don't, you will forever continue to be a victim and at the mercy of the events that come your way. You will be powerless.*

How many times have you heard someone remark, "Why did this happen to me.?" or "How can a loving God allow such suffering and sorrow?" The Universe doesn't allow any bad to happen; it is we who create our own experience and maintain balance and love. Remember, all major events that happen in your lifetime are for your growth and experience, of which you yourself chose to occur. Remember, **life doesn't happen to us; it happens for us.** We have a responsibility to ensure the world is at peace and harmony through our actions. This is responsibility at its most complete vibration. Since we are one with the Universe, if it is out of alignment, then so are we.

I think we all will remember September 11, 2001, when human beings from our own planet purposefully flew airplanes into the World Trade Center towers in New York. One has to ponder how such action could ever be taken by anyone. I do not profess to understand these things but I do know that the humans responsible for this action are also connected to the Oneness. I know that throughout the world people have been conditioned from birth to see themselves and others according to their parents, teachers and religious leaders and most have not been taught that they are one with all of life. If they had known the truth of their Divine Right in life they never would have gone this way. They would only contribute love in the world.

We have this opportunity and responsibility, so become a part of the "critical mass" of a consciousness of love and acceptance. So instead of condemning them, pray for them. Pray for forgiveness of your own anger and contribution to the state of the world. We do not have to like someone's behavior to love their soul. In fact I think we must stand up against ill behavior but it just doesn't look like a fight. It looks like definitive expression and love. When we take it down to such atrocities, and there are many more one could state, it is hard to see that each of us operates out of our need to contribute and our need to love and be loved. We operate according to our understanding of wherever we are in our conscious awareness at any given time. So I implore you to open your mind and your heart to a new way of living; to live a life of love, forgiveness (starting with forgiving yourself) and acceptance.

LOVE AND FORGIVE YOURSELF; LOVE AND FORGIVE OTHERS.

The Super-Conscious is a vast sea of thought powerful enough to create miracles. This aligned thought process equals concentrated power. So, with everything going on in a world where negativity slaps us from all directions, you can allow fear to paralyze you and prevent you from living your truth or not; it is a choice. If you allow worry to take over your thoughts it can cause untold sleepless nights, and anxiety which allows diseases to take over your body; it is understandably difficult to maintain a state of unity when you allow these thoughts to linger.

We all feel alone at times, some more than others, but the overall emotion is the same. This sense of isolation is a needless existence. You are as unlimited as your source, which is unlimited, and you can think yourself into higher, grander, and loftier expressions for expressing more life. When this state is attained you will feel the subtle rebuilding works of God, in whom we live, move and have our being.

If you believe that there is nothing deeper than your conscious mind, then by repeating suggestions of that which you desire, you will likely find it difficult to achieve your highest goals and desires. Most likely you will not discover true fulfillment. The very depth of your being, the self, or "I am" is a spiritual knowing. The "I am", the very foundation of our being upon which we build our mental habitation, is our true essence. We affirm, "I am life," because our soul is eternal life. We affirm, "I am health, peace and perfection," because the real "I", the true individual, the self, is potentially the health and perfection of the Universe.

Before I continue, I'd like to give my disclaimer. Everything in this book is from my point of view. You do not have to believe everything I have written; indeed you do not have to believe anything. If you take at least one thing away with you when you have finished I hope it is an idea of how to start or continue your journey to find true abundance and prosperity in both your professional and personal life. I believe that there is no wrong or right in the way others choose to believe. All I ask is to accept that these are my views and they have the right to co-exist with yours.

One of the age-old questions is, "Who or what is God?" God is the entirety of all that exists. God is not an individual, but rather the Life Force, Universe, Infinite Intelligence, and the Super-Conscious. Having said that, if this is the case, then aren't we all God in expression? This is a difficult concept for most to grasp, but if we are made in God's image then we must be God expressing as individuals. Our God-like self is our higher form of self. Perhaps "God himself" is also a separate expression, if you will, and we know when we are in the presence of God.

The essence of God that is beautiful, loving and desired, all knowing and all possibility is what is available to you now. With this understanding, you are never alone, no matter the circumstance. The Universe is all energy, all life, all beauty and all accomplishments completed. I want you to remember a very important aspect of spirituality: it is about Self; what you think, what you feel, what you know, what you resonate with, who you are. It is very important to take the time to get to know your Self when you embark on your spiritual journey.

Since we are all a part of the Infinite Intelligence, it is important to become self-aware, emotionally and mentally stable. To do this, we must make a conscious decision to become aware of our feelings and thoughts. From this point on, everything you do, you can do from a place of truth, and as a result the outside world will no longer affect you. I believe this awareness stops your reliance on others and increases your ability to give yourself love, acceptance, happiness and peace. Connecting and maintaining communication with the Super-Conscious is crucial to reach your ultimate state of being for this lifetime.

If you are ready to move beyond the traditional sense of believing and the obstacles created by this, it is important to realize that you were given free will in order for you to advance your own spiritual growth; to live your life based on your desires. Only you know where your true path lies as you journey through this life. Unconditional love is the key that unlocks our spiritual and personal growth.

All of us possess, in one degree or another, the ability to make known our gifts and talents. You just need to utilize your natural abilities, and relearn the proper way to communicate with the Infinite Intelligence. Once you connect to this, you will then be able to receive the thought messages, the answers to your questions that pertain to your personal life that you are living at this very moment. We are as one with the Universe, and the sooner we realize this, peace will engulf the planet. It doesn't matter what religion you are, all that matters is what we do with our life.

PRAYER

For those who pray, just know that true prayer is a spiritual action, and when it is done in earnest and with emotion, it will provide introspection, so that looking within yourself leads to becoming aware of not only your inner strengths, but of your imperfections as well. This in turn brings you together with the Infinite Intelligence, which inspires you to endeavor to reach higher levels of attainment.

Prayer is only effective when you are truly inspired and attuned to the creative forces of the Universe. When your soul desires knowledge, awareness, and depth, prayer automatically attracts its answer by creating a vibration that brings those who are in tune with your personal vibration.

GOD HAS NOT GIVEN UP ON YOU, SO WHY WOULD YOU.

Prayer has nothing to do with religion. When you sincerely pray from deep within your very soul, you are connecting with the Infinite Intelligence.

Bargaining with the Universe will only keep you where you are now. Even if you are stuck now you can pray your way clear. My sister Judy once very much wanted to create loving thoughts for her adult children while she was traveling, yet she realized that she herself was not in a grounded, loving place. At that moment she was caught up in her own thoughts that were not going to help her or her children. So she did the best she knew how at that time and asked God for help. Read her story and the results that were created.

"Love is an amazing motivator. Here I was on my way to Utah for my husband's grandchild's baptism and a short fishing trip and I was angry. Angrier than I remember being in a long time. I was turning 50 and I wanted a birthday party back home with all of my friends and family, for sure not to be going on a fishing trip. On his last birthday I had thrown a huge, great, sit-down dinner party with all of his favorite friends; on mine, he was doing absolutely nothing, and it was the big '5 0' for me. I could not even think straight or get off of my attitude. What was I to do? I could not send out good energy into the world so who was going to keep good thoughts for my kids back home? I did the only thing I could think of; I prayed and I prayed and I prayed. I sat in that plane ride pretending to be asleep and just prayed straight for 45 minutes asking God to take care of my kids as I was too angry to hold them in that light. I asked that he send angels to take care of my son and my daughter while I was in this terrible state of mind.

I learned later that at the very time I was in my prayer, my son had fallen asleep at the wheel of his car on his way home from work. With the sun beating in his face and a long day at work, from very early in the morning until that afternoon he had worked and thus coming home he nodded off and the front wheel of his car caught a hole on the side of the road and flipped three-and-a-half times. He did not have his seat belt on and was flipped out the top of the sunroof of his Ford Explorer.

IT IS SAID THAT HOLDING ILL THOUGHTS OF OTHERS IS LIKE TAKING A POISON PILL AND HOPING THE OTHER PERSON DIES.

The guy behind him who saw the accident assumed he would retrieve my son's body from the car. When he walked up, to his astonishment, he saw my son was busy picking up CD's that had been thrown from the car. The guy then said he saw an angel on my son's shoulder, which was the only way, he could understand that my son was alive. God had listened to my prayer and sent an angel to protect my son. Needless to say when they took him to the hospital to examine him, he did not have one scratch on him. He was just upset for falling asleep and wrecking the car. He was sound, healthy and grateful that he was alive."

–Judy Land

So even when you are not in a peaceful, loving, harmonious state of mind, you can ask for help, and if you are willing for your own ego to get out of the way, the Universe will provide.

We don't have to do everything; in fact we cannot. Often the act of letting go is the most powerful action we can take in our lives. In Judy's case, she realized that she was putting out energy that was not in harmony with what she wanted. Her greatest desire was for her kids to be protected. There is no way she could have protected them herself even if she was in town. Because she was away from home her emotions and intentions were heightened. She asked for help and her prayers were answered in a powerful way. You do not have to know how to fix your problems or even change any aspect of your life, but you can always pray with clear intention and emotion. This creates energy in the Universe that does affect change.

DIVINE LOVE

When people are angry and unhappy it is because they are not in touch with their true connection with the Infinite. It is difficult to be truly peaceful, or in harmony, when we do not feel connected to a higher power. It is difficult to believe in yourself at times when you are not aware of your connection to your source. For you to be fulfilled in your quest in life, I suggest you examine what you think is your true purpose in life. Whatever it is, I know it is an expression of true love. Many have the misconception that love is just romantic feelings, physical attraction, or sexual desires. It is so much more; love is the divine force within each of us giving us the most powerful inner strength needed to excel in life.

Everything is love because God is love and God is in everything. Holding on to hate, resentment, anger, disappointments, and jealousy only hurt us. *It is said that holding ill thoughts of others is like taking a poison pill and hoping the other person dies.*

Love is a deliberate act and is your choice whether you love and create harmony in the world. You can make a conscious effort to ensure your actions are moving toward love. Earlier, in chapter 5, we discussed the ever-constant universal laws. If you peel away their layers, you'll find love is a core principle. These universal laws and love are as true now as ever.

When we release those negative emotions our energy is replenished. By letting go and sharing love with those around you, you're helping to create Oneness with others. Now I am not referring to romantic love; instead, I'm referring to divine love. This provides us the opportunity to have the divine experience. Unconditional love multiplies itself exponentially throughout the planet.

WE ALL HAVE THE OPPORTUNITY TO CONTRIBUTE TO THE NEW UNIVERSAL CONSCIOUSNESS.

We do not need others' acceptance or approval because with love it matters only how we are ready to give. We will always get many times more love in return. Love is here in our self; only we need to give it to others.

In order to receive and give love, we must be in a suitable consciousness, one in which unity and inner harmony with ourselves and our surroundings are fulfilled. This is the consciousness in which only positive actions are performed.

One of the best techniques to enter in this state of consciousness is by expressing genuine love toward others.

- Make a list of the people in your life who you have a difficult time loving.
- Think of one simple way you would be comfortable demonstrating your love toward them.
- Create the courage to do it and watch what happens.

THE ESSENCE OF GOD, THAT WHICH IS BEAUTIFUL, LOVING AND DESIRED, ALL KNOWING AND ALL POSSIBILITY IS WHAT IS AVAILABLE TO YOU NOW.

If you can demonstrate love in any way, no matter big or small, you've taken the first step into this elevated level of consciousness. If you find yourself feeling down, maybe so low you just want to end it all; if you will think of one person whose life you could improve, maybe in a small way, and you do it, you will discover life within you and I promise you, you will feel better. We all are here to grow, to give and to celebrate every moment.

Let the power of love bring happiness in your life. Whatever you do, do it with love. Love your career and be rewarded with success. Love your family and live a happy family life. Love your friends and get their blessings. If you give love, you will get back more and more love. Continue to enrich your life and the lives of others with the divine power of love. Extend yourself to helping others; look beyond your current actions. Giving is one of the best ways to experience your connection to the Universe. Only when you know love do you live a fuller, prosperous and meaningful life.

In life the little everyday obstacles are sometimes the most challenging. We can take on our big goals with enthusiasm, joy and love but then sometimes the little frustrations can happen and we go to our smallest place. What do I mean by this? I say I am in a constant state of remembering and forgetting who I am at any point in time. In truth, who we are is infinite potential. We are connected to and one with the Infinite Power, Love and Intelligence. We are always connected to the One Mind.

We are not always aware of our connection, but we are connected just the same. So when I say I am in a constant state of remembering and forgetting who I am, this is what I am referring to. My purpose is to stay in a constant state of awareness of this connection. When we are in this state, we can do anything. We can create anything. We are, in fact, co-creators so we want to stay in a state of awareness and gratitude as much as possible. When we are focused on our dream, we are in a high vibration, centered and grounded. Then the simplest thing can happen, a difference of opinion with our spouse or someone else for example. They disagree with us and we go to our small place, our defensive place, our righteous place. We find it suddenly important to let that person know how wrong he or she is. Very loving, wouldn't you say? This mechanism is a dream killer. It's essential to learn certain disciplines if we are going to be effective in our lives.

Coming from your heart or coming from a loving place is when you get yourself out of the way and allow others to be however they want to be without you taking it personally and letting them know how much you disapprove of them. You could most likely change the whole dynamic, at a moment like that, with a loving statement and perhaps some light humor. When you honor someone when they are acting badly they usually get it right away and it defuses the situation. You didn't make them wrong for being tense or intense at that moment. You just loved them through it. What is interesting is you will feel better no matter how they respond because you didn't give your power away, the power you have over the only thing you have power over and that is your own behavior, your own reaction to whatever comes your way. This is accomplished by being proactive about how you are going to be that day. Live from inside out, not outside in.

SAY GOODBYE TO YOUR HAMMERS

As you wake in the morning, make a conscious choice how you are going to be this day. Choose to receive love and to express love in all that you do. When you notice that you are not coming from that loving place, choose again. I always start my day this way. I choose how I am going to be; loving, clear, understanding, filled with joy, radiant health, and prosperity and I choose to express love in all that I do. Now this is important – when I notice that I am not coming from this loving place, I do NOT get out the hammer and beat myself over the head for not being this way. I simply, notice that I am not being what I said I wanted to be and I choose again right then and there on the spot. This is an act of forgiveness to myself so I can just move on, being who I say I want to be. Michael Beckwith says to start your day by asking yourself these three questions: "How do I grow today, how do I give today and how do I celebrate?"

Remember God is within each of us. The time has truly come for us to evolve higher spiritually. Seek within to find the true wisdom of our loving Universe. Share the wisdom freely with all who seek it. It is not necessary to try to sell it or force it upon others who don't care for the knowledge; give it freely.

Everyone is on their own path and all paths lead to God. Share loving thoughts with everyone everywhere. Those who are ready to receive will. Others may start preparing to receive and give. You may never know how you enhanced someone's life.

Just give and be open to receive gifts of love.

CHAPTER 8
— EMBRACING THE UNFAMILIAR —

*Courage is the power to
let go of the familiar.*

–Raymond Lindquist

8

CHAPTER

Imagine, for a moment, that we are all here on this earth for a particular reason. The Infinite Power has given us all unique gifts and talents to share with the world. Of course to believe this statement would require that you have an implicit understanding that there is something greater than you are, some greater force than we are. Continuing with this line of thinking, it is safe to say that we were not put here for our beliefs; instead we're here for all that we already are. What does this mean? It means that you are perfect, whole and complete.

When I say that you are already perfect, I am really saying that you are this perfect idea, expressing at your current level of awareness. My daughter Kym is a great example of this. She was a perfect idea expressed at her current level of awareness when she and Rod reconnected. In her story in Chapter 1, she referred to the shiny people who she always wanted to be but in reality she was already perfect in her truth. Yet because she viewed herself and others a certain way, she believed she was less than perfect. As Kym evolved and became more aware of her truth, she outshined those who she once watched from a far. Now, Kym serves others as the Executive Director of Human Understanding and Growth Seminars (HUGS) focused on transforming the lives of young people in Eastern Long Island. She uses her truth to help others shine, which is the ultimate act of love.

All you need to create the life you desire is already within you, right here and right now. Nothing is outside of you. You do not have to chase the elusive. Look inside yourself. Your purpose here is self actualization. Self actualization is finding the connection to your inner world with the Infinite and utilizing your untapped talents and gifts. We express our uniqueness in many different ways. For example, we express ourselves by writing, painting, volunteering, working in our jobs or businesses, playing music, raising our children, being with our animals or with nature in anyway, or any other way conceivable.

When you are in tune with your true self and reach a level of self-actualization, you allow others to enjoy your inner being without worry of acceptance, without the need to satisfy people, but simply for the mere joy of self-expression. It is a natural progression when we get out of the way and allow it. The rewards are astounding. You experience a feeling that nothing is left wanting, a sense of freedom and liberation, a sense of total involvement, of self-harmony, a sense of satisfaction that you are an integral part of all that surrounds you; yes, all that surrounds us all.

> THE INFINITE POWER HAS GIVEN US ALL UNIQUE GIFTS AND TALENTS TO SHARE WITH THE WORLD. ALL YOU NEED TO CREATE THE LIFE YOU DESIRE IS ALREADY WITHIN YOU, RIGHT HERE AND RIGHT NOW.

Your conscious mind is wired to filter and judge every idea, experience and association. It is your choice what you do with it. It is always your choice what thoughts you allow to linger in your conscious mind. I know it doesn't always feel like it is your choice but it is. I know that you most likely have chatter that goes on in that mind of yours and it is up to you to direct it and tell it to shut up if necessary. It is up to you to create the picture and thoughts you choose to hold in your mind. The truth is that your key to freedom is to find out who you are in your soul, not in your mind.

IT'S UP TO YOU TO TELL THE CHATTER TO SHUT UP.

You see, the thoughts that you have held, you passed on to your subconscious mind where they became your beliefs. Many of these beliefs were passed on to you by your parents, teachers, ministers and others. The problem with beliefs is we believe they are truth and, subsequently, they do become our reality. So how do we change our reality? We really must take charge of our conscious mind. We must quiet it and search into our soul for our truth. Remember, you are created in perfection with infinite potential. If you need a belief system, why not choose to believe in that; that you are created in perfection with infinite potential? It will get you much further in life than the beliefs you may currently be harboring.

A friend of mine tells of her journey of claiming her freedom in her life after being raised with a particular set of beliefs that just didn't fit for her. This is her story in her own words.

"I knew from a very early age that I was different from my family. I was raised in a strict Catholic family where rules were to be followed without question. All of my life I was told that Catholics just don't think like everyone else and that they are the one true church. I remember as a child hearing my mother talk about her friends whose children left the church and then remark, "I don't know what I would ever do if one of my children joined another church." She always seemed to stare more at me than she did my brother and sister when she said those words. It was almost as if she knew what the future held.

So out of guilt or some misguided sense of obligation, I continued on going through the motions to please my parents and anyone else I deemed important. It wasn't until I had my daughter that I started to question the way I thought. I wasn't happy. Sure there were moments of happiness, but always with an underlying source of sadness. I couldn't explain the way I felt. I just knew that something was off or missing in my life.

The moment I held my daughter for the first time, I changed. I saw this beautiful, perfect creature in my arms. She was so pure and innocent. The only thought I had from that moment on is I don't want her to ever hurt or suffer in any way. Now I know that suffering is inevitable in life, without it we don't learn and grow and there were going to be a lot of areas in her life I couldn't control. I wanted to give her the freedom to think to be herself and most importantly live her life for her not as I had lived to please my family.

To do this, however, I had to reevaluate my own thought processes. It was a difficult journey, but one that I never regretted taking. I soon found what was missing in my life. Me, that was what was lacking, I hadn't found my true self; I lived for others and to please others. I had to make a decision to choose my thoughts and not live according to those of my family.

I began to focus on myself and what made me happy. Over the course of a couple of years, I quit my job, changed careers, and followed my truth. Finally, I felt free and best of all I can give my daughter the gift of freedom. Free to be herself and to find her place in this world."

–Liz Ragland

What is beautiful and inspiring about Liz's story is that she looked inside of herself for her truth. It is not to say that anyone's choice of religion is wrong; it however is a personal choice. Liz did not feel that she was given a choice as a child and she did her best to please the people in her life who were most important to her. When we have our own children, most of us really do examine our lives and beliefs at that point and Liz realized then that she had been living her life by someone else's values and beliefs. There is no joy in life when we do this.

Take a look at your own life and examine it carefully to see whose beliefs you really hold. Are they really yours or did you adopt them unconsciously? That doesn't mean that you cannot adopt them now consciously, but at least it is valuable to determine whose life you are really living. At any point in life, you can choose to adopt consciously the beliefs you currently hold; if they serve you, or if you determine that they do not serve the authentic you, you can replace them. You can simply change your mind about what thoughts you will allow to linger and focus your thoughts on what it is you desire instead of on what appears to be your problems. You can decide at any time the life you wish to live and begin living in your mind that life until it becomes your reality. This exercise is a lifelong process. It is not a twenty-minute affirmation. This is about making a choice each day about how you are going to live your life. How you are going to think, speak and walk in your world.

YOUR CONSCIOUS MIND IS WIRED TO FILTER AND JUDGE EVERY IDEA, EXPERIENCE AND ASSOCIATION.

This applies to every aspect of your life, relationships, finances, health and spirituality. It is important to focus on what you want, not what you don't want. For example, you wish to lose weight. You're focusing on losing your weight and it becomes this vicious circle. You lose weight and then you want to find it again because you continue to see yourself as overweight. Rather than hold the vision of you as heavy, focus and visualize you as healthy, fit and trim. It is simply a Universal Law in that what you focus your energy on will grow. If you want to change your circumstances and situations you must focus your energy and thoughts on that which you do want. So in this case, instead of focusing on losing, you need to focus on health. Start visualizing your body in a lighter, thinner, healthier form. See yourself doing physical activities in alignment with this new shape. See yourself in different clothes, your friends and loved ones acknowledging how great you look. This is just a good example of how your focus can help or harm you.

When we apply this to your finances and relationships, start visualizing the life you want to live. What kind of a home do you want to live in? See yourself living the life wearing the clothes, driving the car, and associate your visions with what you want financially, not with what you have now. Then get ready to do whatever it takes to make that happen. You will attract to you the perfect opportunities to act upon. I appreciate how challenging it can be to hold this vision in the face of what looks like a daunting reality in today's economy. It is important to remember that the way to change your circumstances is through your inner world; *that is the work you do internally*, not the outer world.

LEARN TO QUIET THE CHATTER THAT ARGUES FOR YOUR LIMITATIONS.

If you are seeking a relationship yet you constantly think that there is no one out there who is right for you, guess what, you will be right. If you change your focus to the knowing that there are millions of people on the planet and that you are a wonderful, deserving, giving person and that the right relationship is available now, you will begin to notice all the possibilities around you.

As you look within for answers and discover that, in fact, you are connected to the Life Force; that you do have a soul created with infinite potential, you will find peace and will learn to quiet the chatter that argues for your limitations. It is true that we are all producing less than our infinite potential;

instead we are all producing in the finite. That does not make us less than perfect expressions of the Infinite; it simply means that we are in some kind of a process. Embrace the process. Remember, *it is this journey we have come here to experience.*

It may not seem to you, at this point in life, that peace and harmony are actually a natural state of being but in fact, they are. The turmoil that we often experience is not our natural state but a manufactured state of being. The good news is, because you did manufacture it, you can re-craft it. You have the power to simply let it go at any point in time. There is a wonderful training program called the Sedona Method that focuses on just this kind of work. It suggests that you can embrace the thoughts that bring you pain and at any moment simply let them go. You can go and retrieve them at any time you choose. The power of the exercise is you will eventually begin to see that you are in fact in complete control of your experience every moment of every day. This is a pretty powerful thought, wouldn't you say? It is powerful and more importantly, it is true.

We have all, in our lives, created beliefs that cause us to be in a particular state of being that is familiar to us. We seem to gravitate back to our false truth when we are under any kind of perceived pressure. Having said that, we can learn to alter this familiar state and adopt a new more peaceful and productive state of being.

START VISUALIZING THE LIFE YOU WANT TO LIVE.

Do you remember in Chapter 4 we talked about our human needs? Tony Robbins does extensive work in this area and I have found it most useful when working with my clients. We talked about the fact that underlying everything we say and do we are attempting to have our needs met. This goes for all of us. We all have a need for certainty, we all need some variety or spice in our lives, we all have a need for love or connection with others and we all need to feel significant. Those are basic functioning needs that we will find a way to have met no matter what, but what I have discovered and I share with you now is, if we focus our attention and energy on the only two needs that actually bring us a sense of fulfillment we automatically satisfy the first four needs.

As a reminder, those two needs are so simple and are the breath of life for our souls. They are *personal growth and contribution to others*. Think of it, how simple life can be. How rewarding and fulfilling and so very peaceful and harmonious life could be if only we would focus our attention each day on our personal growth and on finding ways to contribute to others. Michael Beckwith would add, find ways to celebrate each day as well. I really like celebration for I think we often forget to rejoice in life. *Life is a gift and all the challenges are our gifts as well.* People ask me all the time how do I do this? How do I stop the chatter? How do I change my life from what I experience now to a better life? It does take discipline, which Webster defines as activity, exercise, or a regimen that develops or improves a skill. I am not saying that you magically change everything overnight, but you really can make a huge shift right here and now with a decision to honor who you are in

REMEMBER, IT IS THE JOURNEY WE HAVE COME HERE TO EXPERIENCE.

your truth as an expression of a greater power and focus on being all that you can be and on contributing to others each day of your life. It really is magical.

Start with your closest loved ones. Sometimes we treat them the worst, don't we? We will be polite to strangers and snap at our loved ones. This seems so very backward if you think about it. Not that we should be snapping at strangers either for they too are connected to the Infinite Power and to us as well. But I think you know what I mean. We have those people who we have attracted into our lives, either by birth or marriage and they are involved in our lives and would likely lay their lives down for us, yet we often treat them as if they do not matter to us. We often snap at them and otherwise abuse them with our inconsiderate actions. So let's start right here when learning about contribution to others. How can we make their day a little better? Ask yourself the question, "What does this person need from me today?" You will be amazed that not only do you brighten their day but you will feel better inside. You will automatically have all your needs met as you press yourself for improvement and contribute to others. Try it now.

> IF YOU FEEL DEPLETED WHEN YOU GIVE, IT WAS NOT REALLY A GIFT.

Giving of yourself to others is probably the fastest way I know to feel a sense of connection to self and to something greater than your ego. Be clear that I am not speaking of giving at your own personal depletion. I am speaking of always giving from the heart that which brings you joy to give. You should always gain more from the act of giving.

You should never feel depleted. **If you feel depleted when you give, it was not really a gift.** It may have been an attempt at some kind of manipulation. It may have been that you hoped someone would think better of you for doing it. This is not true giving; let me be clear about that.

THE INFINITE POWER AND FORCE HAS CREATED ALL THAT LIFE IS AND YOU ARE A PART OF IT.

Maybe you already feel depleted and do not feel that you have anything to offer another. If you honestly believe this way, I must be firm in telling you, it simply is not true about you or any other person. It is important that you are clear that you are a perfect expression of the Infinite Power and Intelligence, as you. If you are having difficulty relating to this statement, go to a quiet place where you will not be disturbed, then close your eyes and take some deep breaths. I want you to acknowledge the fact that you are connected to this power and that you are grateful for the knowing that it works through you. Keep looking into your heart. Get out of your head and feel the love move through you.

Dr Harry Morgan Moses says "If Life is not showing you Magic, you're not looking for it."

When you quiet your mind and open your heart you will begin to know that it is true. I ask you to trust that sense that comes to you as truth. You are capable of anything that you can accept into your life. It is necessary that you know you are deserving, no matter what you have manifested into your reality so far. The Infinite Power and Force has created all that life is and you are a part of it. You are essential. All that you are is a gift to the rest of life. When you truly understand this you will find it easier to give of your true essence to others and in doing so will create peace, harmony, love and prosperity into your own life.

CHAPTER 9

— TO BE OR NOT TO BE —

And God said, you are not human doings, you are human beings.

–Jeri Walz

9
CHAPTER

How many of us wake up every day and think about what we have to do today? The word "do" is embedded in our psyche from childhood. Remember our parents telling us to do our chores, do our homework, do our best, etc.? And remember this one, "What are you going to do when you grow up?" When we messed up, remember the words, "What are you going to do about it?" We were constantly measured on what we do. No wonder as adults we fill our time in a state of doing and measure our success by what we have done.

Unfortunately, many of us were never encouraged as a child to create a purpose for our life, a sense of beingness. What makes things worse is that so many of the things we have done in our life are based upon poured-in beliefs from childhood. These beliefs have orchestrated what we were supposed to do to be loved, accepted and successful. It's much like that hamster on the wheel going round and round thinking this is progress while still imprisoned in the cage. We are not proud of some of the things we've done and we suffer for it. So how do we break free of this cycle?

IT IS ALL ABOUT OUR "BEINGNESS"

Imagine for a moment a glass goblet and that each thing you have done in your life, and each thing that _you perceived_ was done to you, is an ice cube in that goblet. Think of these ice cubes as the "content" in your life and think of yourself as the holder of this content and ask yourself, "How are you holding the content?"? By this I mean, in what context are you holding your life? This context is your state of "being", in other words, your state of mind and state of heart. Imagine now that these ice cubes melt into a mixed blend and become a theme that you live by. For purposes of illustration, some of us have a theme that our life works and is blessed, while others may have a theme that life is hard and disappointing. The amazing thing about either theme is that it is a powerful attractor that will determine your destiny and quality of your life. If this is true, then wouldn't it be smart to shift your state of being in how you hold your life if you are not happy or not getting the results you want?

For those of you who are parents, this is an especially important concept and critical to your child's life experience. The amazing thing is that if you shift your beingness, then everything in the goblet shifts with you. For example, let's say that you have had experiences in your life that ended up as a theme that life is tough. Now, you may be unaware that you are coming from that state of being; in fact most of us don't even notice that we are coming from any particular state. Yet, it always ends the same. We feel victimized and strangely righteous about it when sharing with others. There is this story about a woman who had a theme in her life that she was always sick and made sure others always

ALWAYS CHECK IN FIRST WITH HOW YOU ARE GOING TO "BE" BEFORE DECIDING WHAT YOU ARE GOING TO "DO" IN ANY SITUATION.

knew it. When she died, her tombstone righteously read, "I told you I was sick."

Imagine if she would have shifted her beingness to hold all her illnesses as an opportunity to grow and create a new purpose in her life. We hear of people who do exactly this. Someone gets a disease and then starts raising awareness and funding for its cure. Michael J. Fox, the actor, is a perfect example of this. Certainly, his Multiple Sclerosis (MS) may have changed his ability to do the acting that he used to do, yet by shifting his beingness, his life unfolded with greater purpose and fulfillment.

Shifting your state of mind and your state of heart is a choice. Imagine your life if you chose to believe that everyone that did something negative to you, and everything negative that has happened to you, was a learning experience. It is just "what is" and how you reacted to it was a choice. My husband Rod was fortunate years ago to facilitate a "conscious-raising group" on an ongoing basis with women. Most of the women were single parents and he kept hearing a complaining theme about ex-husbands who didn't show up for the kids and didn't keep their money agreements regarding child support.

SHIFTING YOUR STATE OF MIND AND YOUR STATE OF HEART IS A CHOICE.

He created an exercise where he had them close their eyes and imagine an "asshole" (pardon my French). He waited till all the women had someone in mind. Why don't you do this now; just play along. Think of someone who you always react to; you wish you could control your reaction to but you don't seem able to do so. It could be a relative, a boss, or an ex-spouse. Do you have someone in mind? For most of Rod's participants, it was their ex-husband. He would then ask the women to imagine they had died, passed through, and were sitting with God in full knowledge that they had passed on. Sitting next to God was the "asshole".

In bewilderment, each asked God what the "asshole" was doing here. God warmly put arms around the "asshole", leaned forward and said, "This is your teacher. This was my gift to you; I sent this person to you as your teacher. How did you do?" The looks on the women were worth remembering as they flashed through their past experiences with the "asshole". Throughout the following sessions, the women shared with joy the breakthroughs they were having about themselves and also reported on the positive shift in the men's behavior as a result. All that occurred was that these women shifted their beingness (state of mind and state of heart). In other words, they shifted the context of how they held their ex-husbands. The bonus was that by shifting their beingness, it not only affected the future but also affected their internal spiritual relationship with their past. I encourage you to do this process if you didn't already. Close your eyes and do the same process these women did using whoever the "asshole" is in your life. Really feel God speaking to you about your teacher and choose to release the feelings about this person and embrace the lessons.

Remember when I talked earlier about how the individual events (ice cubes) melt and get blended into a theme, the beauty about shifting your beingness/context is that all the blended events are affected, at some level, in one fell swoop. How great is that!!!

Throughout my life, I've learned that by shifting my state of mind and state of heart, my life gets enriched. Even though in boarding school, when I felt alone and abandoned, I did not understand what shifting my beingness meant; however I was able to do so, instinctively, and my world opened up to me. Always check in first with how you are going to "be" before deciding what you are going to "do" in any situation. It is your state of mind and state of heart that attracts and drives your results. This applies to every event or activity in your life. If you ask the question of yourself, "How am I going to **be** with this person or in this situation?" you will go into it feeling grounded.

WHEN WE FOCUS ON "DOING" WE OFTEN JUST GO THROUGH THE MOTIONS AND THIS CAN CREATE MANY UNNECESSARY CHALLENGES.

When we ask ourselves, "What am I going to **do** in this situation?" can you feel the difference in your level of tension? A friend of mine recently called me for counsel regarding her relationship with her long-term boyfriend who, in her mind, had disappointed her significantly and she felt hurt and let him know it. He broke off communication so she was asking me, "What do I need to do?" Think about this man. He had no way to win in this scenario and now felt responsibility for her unhappiness. How dreary for a guy is that? So, I had her close her eyes and ask herself, with what she knows about this man, does he love you and would he intentionally hurt you? She responded he loves me and that he would never intentionally hurt me. With this realization of the truth, she shifted her state of mind and state of heart about him. She recognized that she was making up the hurt in her own mind based upon old beliefs. She also discovered that she had not adequately communicated her expectations to him, which affected his behavior in this particular situation.

When we focus on "doing" we often just go through the motions and this can create many unnecessary challenges. Think about a situation that you may be facing now and ask yourself how you choose to be in this moment. If you are facing something difficult and you are worrying what you should do; change the question around and ask yourself, "How do I want to be? How do I want to be when I am with a particular person or how do I want to be in this particular situation?" You decide how you are going to be. Don't let the other person or the situation determine how you are going to react.

In your career, for example, you may not be satisfied and you may not be earning the kind of money you wish to make, yet you are very busy "doing" and by doing so you may not have created the time to find your soulmate, or create a beautiful relationship with the one who is in your life now. Instead, why not "be" and allow those people, places, and situations to flow freely in your life? When we are willing to just "be" we are in alignment with the Universe and whatever ways and means our desires are manifested, we will know it is how it is supposed to be. We then are not attached to it. We didn't "push" through it, to "endure" it, to "get through" to the end. When we are so attached to the end result it is exhausting and even if it comes together, any satisfaction is only fleeting.

When we are grounded in our "beingness" and allow the universe to work, we expect things to work out and they do. They may not always look the way you thought they would but you realize that it is all perfect and you needn't question its perfection. Your beingness will point the way to what you need to do next. To embrace this concept is huge and will absolutely empower results more to your liking. In a nutshell, by shifting how you hold something in your mind and heart to a higher vibration spiritually, you attract from the Universe the things to do based upon your beingness. In other words, you will attract exactly what you want, based on your state of mind and state of heart.

You may not always get what you think you want but you absolutely get what you believe. It is important to take responsibility for your thoughts. This is where pure personal accountability, like rubber, hits the proverbial road. Your embedded beliefs are what you manifest. So if you want something different than what you have created so far, it is your beingness that needs to shift; and because there is a gestation period, you might want to start shifting your beingness NOW!!!!!

The exciting news is that we do have the ability to maintain a state of fulfillment throughout any circumstance and receive the full benefits of the potential for our growth. Embrace that there is a reason for these circumstances and your job is to discover those reasons so that your next steps may be unfolded before you. In the absence of this shift in beingness, the Universe is left with vague responses based upon your inherited old beliefs and without you even realizing it, you will accept the results in a mindset of complacency.

Our experiences do not have to be fraught with worry or anxiety. We can accomplish what we want with little effort when we take comfort in knowing that whatever happens is meant to happen and will, ultimately, be in our best interest. Now, I'm not telling you that you won't ever experience discomfort; in fact, you must be willing to get uncomfortable if you are going to grow. There is no growth if you constantly stay in what is familiar and comfortable to you. What I am saying, however, is that when you do encounter what may feel like adversity in life, you'll have the wisdom to embrace it because there is a very specific reason for it. Once we learn to "be" all of the trivial aspects of life tend to fall away. We know that there is a greater meaning for our existence and life holds so much for you if you will only choose to allow it. A quote that illustrates this concept is Paul J. Meyer's, **"Whatever you vividly imagine, ardently desire, sincerely believe and enthusiastically act upon. . . must inevitably come to pass."**

Before we go any further, I'd like to take the opportunity to dispel a myth that many people believe will help change their lives. There is no such thing as luck. A dear friend of mine once said, "Those who believe in luck usually get it, and it's mostly bad". A successful entrepreneur whose business grosses over a million dollars in the first year isn't lucky. This person believes in him or herself, takes hold of the reins and doesn't look back. Luck has nothing to do with our triumphs in life. A strong sense of self and the knowledge that anything is possible is the determining factor for whether you live in survival mode or

THERE IS NO SUCH THING AS LUCK.

flourish and prosper. The best definition I have heard for luck is, *"when preparedness meets with opportunity."* If you study the people considered to be lucky you will find that they had defined what they wanted, prepared their state of mind and state of heart and plowed ahead with unwavering passion and motivation.

I want to help you get the most out of your life. Life is meant to be lived with energy, fueled by inspiration, and lived with the understanding that there are no limits. Stop and think about the magnitude of this. What would happen if you lived life to the fullest and spent every day as if it were your last one? By consciously "being" in a state of mind that supports you, you will exceed your own expectations and live a life you never knew imaginable. First, however, you have to examine who you are and what you truly want. It is important that you understand where you are right now in terms of your consciousness.

If you want to know where you are, what you believe up until this point, what you have been thinking about, look around you and see what you have manifested into your life so far; this is your current level of consciousness. Where do I live, who are my friends, what do I do for a living, how is my weight, how much money do I earn in a year, how much money have I invested in my personal growth, what kind of intimate relationship have I attracted, what is my contribution to others, etc. etc.? Just notice your answers without judgment. Remember, you created your current state based upon past beliefs and past states of mind and heart.

If you want to enhance your life into a greater expression of you, it might be useful to start defining who you choose to be from this moment forward. Stop listening to the world and others and fully begin to embrace your ability and power to decide what is a good life, both

ACTION IS ABSOLUTELY REQUIRED TO BE SUCCESSFUL.

personally and professionally, in your mind? Embed in your heart and soul that a good life contains five elements; your health, spiritual life, relationships, intellectual and financial well-being. They all play a part; in certain stages of our lives some are more dominant.

Focus your beingness and actions on that part that is most urgent to you now, and then continue in the long term, to bring balance to all five. You are capable of achieving anything you desire. I know that it might be difficult to believe at first because you might be living with a "doing" mindset. Your beingness will point the way to what you need to do next. Your state of mind and state of heart will absolutely affect the actions that show up next. I know you know this, so express yourself with your God-given talents and gifts. Action is absolutely required to be successful and sometimes I tell myself and others to just do something; that you can't steer a parked car. But let it be out of inspiration or intention. Most people are running around, doing their lives, with little thought to how they are being. Do not be attached to the results for they are exactly what they are meant to be. Remember, God's intention was for you to be a human being, not a human doing.

LIVING INTERNALLY

Wayne Dyers says, "I cannot always control what goes on outside, but I can always control what goes on inside." Most of us are brought up to look to outside sources for our happiness; a promotion, new car, one new relationship after another, etc.? Do these give you long-term fulfillment or are they just a temporary boost? Your happiness may be nothing more than a fleeting moment.

When we set goals, we do this because we think those things will make us happy, but the truth is, once we accomplish that goal, and acquire whatever it is we went after, what happens? We are just on to the next thing in life. The thing we acquired only gave us a momentary sense of satisfaction. The true joy and fulfillment actually comes in the growth that is required of us to move from one level of consciousness to the next. It is about who you had to become to accomplish that goal. It is about your beingness and had little to do with your doingness. Of course you did things that you likely never did before, but that was the effect of your change in being, as you changed your thoughts and beliefs about yourself and the world around you.

In my personal life I have made far too many choices based on what I thought other people expected of me. To need outside response or validation to feel good, successful or happy turns your life into a roller coaster. You think you will be happy if you get the raise, the extra bonus, or meet someone new, – but you are constantly looking for other ways to give you the feeling of satisfaction and contentment. This can be exhausting mentally, physically and emotionally.

Like most people I too lived externally for the early years of my life. I grew up longing for a loving family. I experienced so many expectations and accepted norms in the world that kept me from seeing my true potential. I didn't follow my own truth, or move toward my own dreams.

I felt I had to achieve and perform in order to be loved; the problem was I didn't know how to do this. I had thoughts and questions that I didn't know anyone in whom I could confide to find the answers and solutions. The beauty I discovered, over time, is the answers were within me all along. I decided to take myself on and achieve all that I could, asking only the experts in their field for professional advice and studying Metaphysics for my personal growth.

> YOU MAY NOT ALWAYS GET WHAT YOU THINK YOU WANT BUT YOU ABSOLUTELY GET WHAT YOU BELIEVE.

My life became my own when I made the decision to take time to discover what I really wanted; as a result, I found areas that filled me with passion and energy. When was the last time you asked yourself what you really want to do? What are your dreams, your passions, and what do you want your legacy to be? When you reach the last days of your life and look back, will you be able to say that you lived your dreams? Will you be able to say that you became all you were meant to become? Did you contribute all that you could? Will you move into the next experience with a sense of fulfillment that you gave all that you had to this life and to your relationships, including your family?

Living your life on an internal level brings a new dimension into you. True achievement and happiness stems from inspiration and "being". Being inspired and going after your dreams and goals, no matter what your colleagues, family or peers are doing, is the mark of living internally. In any area of life you can meet people truly inspired by what they do. It shows through their passion, their service and their attitude. Just imagine the difference between jumping out of bed eager to go to work every day and looking forward to an exciting day doing the things you love versus dragging your feet to work and hoping the day will soon end, or worrying that you might not meet the high and challenging expectations at work – even though that job might be very well paid or with a high status.

THERE IS NO GROWTH IF YOU CONSTANTLY STAY IN WHAT IS FAMILIAR AND COMFORTABLE TO YOU.

It wasn't until I attended PSI 7, a powerful seminar presented by PSI Seminars designed to have me see how I was operating in my life, that I took a look at my life in a new way. I realized in this seminar that I was wired to believe, although not consciously, that nothing I did was ever going to be enough. It really didn't matter if I succeeded or failed at something, I never thought I had done it well enough. With this discovery, I looked back at my life and realized that I had accomplished many things.

There were many great achievements in my business career, my riding and competing with horses, personal and professional awards, unique projects and numerous personal accomplishments. I was physically fit and had great relationships with my husband, family, co-workers and friends. Yet, with all that, I held myself as not enough. It was a shock for me to realize this about myself. If you had asked me what I thought about myself, I thought I held myself in fairly high esteem but I realized that so much of what I had accomplished was out of me trying to build up a long list so that someday I could look at it and feel okay

> YOU CAN RE-WRITE YOUR STORY AND FIND FULFILLMENT IN YOUR LIFE, RIGHT HERE AND NOW.

about myself. The things I had done never really brought me fulfillment, only temporary satisfaction because I had to hurry up onto the next thing so that I could continue to build my list of accomplishments, so that someday, I could look at it and be okay with me.

When I saw this trap clearly, I sat down and wrote out many of my accomplishments, gave myself a pat on the back, said "good for me" and then looked to see that it was never really about the accomplishments at all but the person who I had to become to accomplish the next level. I realized that the true accomplishment was that I was willing to get uncomfortable and grow so that I could take on more. That is the person I could feel good about. Through this exercise I finally fell in love with this woman called Jeri. I no longer feel the need to chase accomplishments; instead, I am inspired to grow and take myself on in greater and greater ways. In this way, I feel fulfillment in all that I do.

What about you? Are you running around trying to accomplish things so that you can feel better about yourself and feel worthy of being loved? <u>You are worthy of being loved right now. You are enough right here and now.</u> I encourage you to write out your list of accomplishments and notice how you had to grow as a person in order to accomplish the next thing. Give yourself credit for this. Give yourself a pat on the back for all that you have done and mostly fall in love with the brave soul who was willing to keep on going and growing. When you finally acknowledge yourself with love, you can begin to free yourself up to motivate from inspiration instead of chasing the elusive next win. Like me, you can rewrite your story and find fulfillment in your life, right here and now.

My dear friend Teresa Mendoza, who worked for me for almost twenty years, is an inspiration to me. She grew up in a Mexican-Catholic culture and always felt suppressed. Even though we had a language barrier, I always shared with her the concepts in the book whenever we were together. Teresa resonated with them and sought me out for more. Rod and I invited her to attend the PSI Basic Seminar, which is very experiential and designed for you to discover what got poured into your life. That course was like a catalyst for Teresa's discovery of the truth within her.

Shortly after she took the course, Rod and I moved to Idaho and Teresa was left without a support network. She held this vision of finding the right support system until one day she opened her purse and found a business card for the minister of the Center For Spiritual Living which embodies the principles in this book and whose theme is: one God, many paths. She had no recollection of how that card got into her purse, but she took action and followed her intuition and called. Soon after, Teresa joined the church and began studying Metaphysics.

Over the course of four years, she completed all of the courses to qualify her for becoming a practitioner of the church. Teresa is the first person to take the test in the Spanish language. As she has grown and developed in her belief and knowing, her family and friends' lives have been enriched as well. Teresa's story is powerful because she shifted her beingness to a more open, perfect embodiment. Initially, she didn't think she had anything to contribute and now she teaches others, in her culture, to do the same.

LIFE IS MEANT TO BE LIVED WITH ENERGY, FUELED BY INSPIRATION, AND THE UNDERSTANDING THAT THERE ARE NO LIMITS.

You no longer need to live a do, have, and be lifestyle, which is living from the outside-in. You can choose right now to honor who you are and choose your happiness now. In order to live a life that brings a true sense of meaning, purpose, and deep fulfillment you need to live a "be, do, have and contribute" lifestyle, or in other words, live from the inside-out. Living this kind of life requires you to be and reflect upon what is most important to you and what brings you the greatest sense of passion. Then you do those things in order to have those experiences.

If you are certain to always be conscious of not only how it contributes to your life, but how it contributes to the lives of others, including friends, family, coworker, and your community at large, you begin to see the vision of who you

> LIVING YOUR LIFE ON AN INTERNAL LEVEL BRINGS A NEW DIMENSION INTO YOU.

were meant to be. As that vision becomes clearer, you will begin to see the path, the way, the doing part of the equation.

I encourage you, from time to time, to take some quiet time away from all those things that fill your day with doingness and think about your life's vision. Think about what you always wanted to be and what you always wanted to accomplish. We all have something; however, it is often buried in a pile of subconsciously driven "buts" and perceived roadblocks that suppress you from achieving what makes you really happy. Ask yourself if there ever would be a right time, and then visualize your life as if the time was now. Imagine how it will feel to be living and breathing your life the way you want it. See yourself passionate about your vision, being up at odd hours of the night writing and planning for the life directed by you; then release this vision to the Universe and follow the paths that unfold.

My life has been full of these quiet moments where I would visualize my life the way I wanted it to be. Being in alignment with the Universal Laws we covered in Chapter 5 has brought to me a life of fulfilled dreams. Others who I have had the honor of coaching and others who I have attracted in my life, who understand and live in harmony with these principles, have also found their life's blessing by becoming more of who they authentically were meant to be.

When you are living your life from the inside-out, your life becomes much simpler. You will intuitively know how you want to spend your time and you will not be distracted by what is not important to you. When you are living from the outside-in, your life is complex. You will be constantly distracted by what is not important to you because you will be constantly searching for something to make you happy.

Making decisions and setting goals becomes easy once you ask yourself if what you are thinking about is in alignment with what is most important to you. Reality is, in my life, I don't really set goals. That may sound very counter to the message many speak to about setting goals, but I really don't set goals. I have a vision that is so clear, of whom I choose to be, what I want and where I am going, that it is like a train I couldn't stop if I tried. I wake in the morning looking forward to my life for I know, each day, that I will be growing personally in the way that I need to, I will take every opportunity that presents itself to me and I will be contributing to someone today. <u>Whoever shows up in my life that day was meant to be with me and I with them.</u> I know I will make a difference, even if it is only in a very small way. I will make a difference today. And by the way, when I realize, on any day, that I forgot to maintain this high vibration, I simply choose again to be that high vibration without any personal hammer on myself for forgetting.

In your life, if what is in front of you seems to be important, great; go ahead with it. If it isn't, that is great too, because you will not have wasted your time and energy. There is a tremendous difference between "have to" and "want to". Are your actions based on your true desire or because you feel they are something you believe you have to do? <u>My recommendation is to immediately eliminate the words "have to" and "had to" right out of your vocabulary,</u>

right along with "can't". These words are not empowering;
they are dream-killers. Remember that you do not "have
to" do anything you do not choose to do. You will certainly
have consequences for your choices, but they may be good
consequences.

> TRUE
> ACHIEVEMENT
> AND HAPPINESS
> STEMS FROM
> INSPIRATION
> AND "BEING".

By living according to be, do, have
and contribute, rather than do, have and
be, you'll soon find that all aspects of
your life will improve exponentially.

Aligning my reflection with my results
has truly changed my life. It was not
always easy for me to move in a different
direction, but now I'm invigorated and
find it exhilarating. I want you to feel
the same sense of inspiration and energy
that I feel. Now is the time for you to turn your potential
into performance. Living internally allows you to achieve
your financial goals and create the love of your life. *Imagine
the effect it would have on your life if you gave yourself the
freedom to find your true reflection and just "be".*

I would like to offer you a simple prayer to start your
day. Add to it in any way that you choose. Think of the
ways you would like to show up this day and add them to
the prayer. Choose how you want to be each day and state
that you choose it. The most important point of the prayer,
other than you experiencing your truth, is the part about
when you notice that you are not being the way you said you
want to be; simply choose again on the spot. Please don't go
and get out the old hammer and start beating yourself up
because you are not being how you said you want to be.
Simply choose again right then and there.

Choosing how we are going to be is a great and effective way to start every day and every event. My husband Rod says, when you choose how you are going to be, it is hard to choose to be a jerk. Well he often uses a more frank expression, but you get the idea. Have fun with it. Make it your own.

> I know that I am one with the One Mind, the Infinite Power and Intelligence and I know that it works through me; I give thanks for this knowing. I know that who I am is spirit, always connected to others and with the Infinite; I am so grateful for this knowing. I am clear about my Purpose and I live each day on Purpose, passionate about my personal growth and contribution to others.
>
> I give thanks for my Divine Right to choose my experience every moment of every day, and in this moment I choose Joy, Love, Radiant Health, Prosperity and I choose to express Love in all that I do and when I notice I am not coming from this place of Harmony and Love, I simply choose again.
>
> I release my word into the Universe knowing that it is done and complete – AND SO IT IS.

CHAPTER 10
— A LOVE STORY ABOUT MONEY —

*Genius of any kind is the ability and
willingness to leave the known world
behind and explore new territory.*

–Karla McLaren

10
CHAPTER

What we create stems from our thinking. Everything that exists due to invention does so because someone thought about it first. Each of us has the ability to choose big, beautiful, prosperous thoughts, or we can choose small, angry, limiting thoughts. With our conscious mind we choose our thoughts, and we can accept or reject any thought we have. Interestingly too, our thoughts are what cause our emotions. As we discussed in the previous chapters, so many of us spend our life letting others control our emotions. After I read a wonderful book by David Hawkins called *"Power vs. Force"* I had an amazing experience that demonstrated this fact to me in vivid color and definition.

Rod and I were living in Idaho at the time and we liked running together in the forest, or when we would visit our son Wes at his house in Eagle, Idaho, we would run through his neighborhood and through a public park where there was a skateboard park and BMX Bike Park along with country trails and more. Rod needed to have back surgery so we stayed at Wes' during that time and while Rod was in the hospital I had a terrible nightmare that was so clear; I can still see it vividly in my mind. It included a man that was going to do me terrible harm and death. It woke me up in a sweat. I shook it off and thought I was over it, but when I brought

Rod home from the hospital after his surgery I went out for a run by myself. As I was running through the neighborhood and down the road toward the park I noticed that I was becoming more and more nervous. I was beginning to fill with fear. I knew that I would be running through the Public Park and then onto a deserted street leading to a trail that would take me through a completely isolated area before it would eventually bring me back through the park and on home from there.

As I could feel the fear building within my body I realized at one point that it was only my thoughts that were causing the fear. It was not based in reality; it was based on my thoughts alone. I began seeing the face of the man in the nightmare and I feared for my life. When

WHAT WE CREATE STEMS FROM OUR THINKING.

I came to grips with the fact that it was only my thoughts causing the fear I realized again in that moment that I could choose to change my thoughts right then and there. I began expressing the truth that I am one with the Infinite Power and Love; that this power and love works and moves through me; that this body that I inhabit is not me at all. It is a body that is on loan to me and who I am in truth cannot be harmed. Even if someone jumped out of the bushes and slit my throat, who I am cannot be harmed. Yes, this body could be killed but not who I am.

As I had these new thoughts of truth of who I am, I was suddenly struck, like a bolt of lightning, and the reality of this truth hit me. Suddenly I felt out of this body. My body felt strong and powerful. As I stepped off the curb to the isolated street, I began running like I have never run before. I felt free and strong. I also felt if someone with bad intentions showed up, I was so connected, I could support them in seeing who they really are in their truth, as well. It really didn't matter at that point. I ran pain-free with a strength and joy I had never experienced before. I ran down the street and up onto the trail through the countryside and back into the park. As I ran back into the park, I saw boys jumping their bikes and their skateboards and realized that they too are a reflection of me. They were just another expression of the One.

In essence that was me in another form. Look how much fun I was having. As I ran across the grass, I could hear it so loudly in my ears. The birds, the trees, everything was enhanced. What a remarkable experience I had that day. All because I opened myself up to the possibility of being connected at a greater level and recognizing my true self. I realized that my thoughts were holding me down to the earthly experience I had always known and I opened myself fully to my true potential in that moment. As I did, my prayer was answered with an experience I will never forget. I have never fully experienced that again but I will always have its memory and I can call upon that memory any time I need to remind myself of my truth.

On a more down-to-earth experience, my husband Rod's story is a good example of what can happen when we are willing and ready to let go of our early beliefs and adopt and embrace new thought that supports us in our true desire in life. Rod's initial consciousness regarding himself, his place in the world and his belief about money was honed in Brooklyn, New York, as the youngest of six children, in a strict Catholic family.

While he loved growing up in the fifties, he became aware, years later, how strongly it had limited his thought-consciousness by his blind acceptance of the beliefs that were poured into him at a very young age. His mother was bedridden most of Rod's life and, after his older siblings moved out, he was the primary caregiver for her. He also met a girl, at age 13, who he felt responsible for and subsequently dated no one else and married her right after he graduated college. He had never questioned that he might have a choice in his life. He lived out of a sense of duty and accepted, without question, the beliefs that were handed down to him in every area of life, including beliefs about people with money.

Fresh out of college, he married the girl he dated since age 13 out of a sense of obligation. Like the other siblings in his family, he stayed clear of entering the business world and, in his case, became a teacher. At age 22, feeling like his life was not his, he had a fortunate encounter with a fellow teacher who, after hearing his life story, asked him why he had to accept his life the way it was. He vehemently resisted and said, "You don't get to ask why about your life, you just have to accept it." Well, he had an epiphany that night and for the first time, ever, Rod began to question why he had to accept the life he felt obligated to live for others. He suddenly realized that he had to be willing to step away from everything he believed in – yes, everything. He intuitively understood that if he tried to get selective, that he would be dragged back into old patterns. Rod made significant and painful decisions to change his life's course and the fruits of his courage began to harvest. At 24 years of age, he was appointed as the Dean of Students in a troubled inner-city high school in Brooklyn, New York.

ATTRACTION IS ALWAYS AT WORK AND YOU WILL ATTRACT THAT WHICH YOU BELIEVE IN.

On paper, he was too young and ethnically challenged yet something inside was blossoming and he discovered a passion for making a difference in the lives of others based upon his intuitive appreciation for the best in all of us. He helped start a program based upon the principle that every one of us inherently wants to make a difference and contribute. What he and his fellow involved teachers found was that, even in this very tough inner-city reactive environment, when a troubled student was given the opportunity and invitation to contribute to others, miracles happened and breakthroughs occurred.

He eventually decided to move to California to pursue teaching there. Life threw him a twist whereby he could not get hired as a teacher, even though he had a successful background in New York. He decided that he might take a shot at sales. This was foreign territory for his soul as he had no background or experience in creating money and wealth by his work product. What a culture shock for him. He now had an opportunity to face a whole new side of himself that he had never looked at before. I am going to let Rod tell you how he had his money breakthrough, in his own words. It is a powerful story that I hope you will read from your own perspective. Personalize the steps and thoughts he went through to see if you can create a breakthrough for yourself. Your story will be different but the principles are the same. Here is Rod's story of his transformation, after moving to California, in his own words:

A LOVE STORY ABOUT MONEY

"When I was growing up, I had always had a vision that my wife, the love of my life, was on the planet but how would I find her. I knew she was here but to find her at a circus in San Diego, CA, who knew! Yes, a woman I was interested in named Judy, who also had two kids, invited me to join her at the circus. Unbeknownst to me, Judy had also invited her sister Jeri to join her. At the circus, Jeri and I had an enriched conversation about life, etc.; however; that was all there was between us. I didn't see Jeri again until a year later when she and I attended the same party. Jeri and I recognized each other and I found myself drawn to her. She had invited a male friend of hers, who was going through a tough divorce, to join her at the party. He started disclosing to me how angry he was with his wife who was already in another relationship; so I took it upon myself to share with him some different perspectives.

As an example, amongst other thoughts, I encouraged him to support his soon-to-be ex-wife by wishing her well and supporting her having what she wants in life and that by doing so, his life would open up and he would get what he wants in his life. I stepped away for a moment while he confided privately to Jeri what an idiot he thought I was. In the meantime, something magical was happening between Jeri and me. Her date was now an intermediary conversation through which I could declare my true self to Jeri. Although, Jeri and I never spoke a word, the energy between us grew more vibrant as I shared more and more with her date. When he stepped away for a moment, feeling the energy between us I turned to Jeri put my arms around her and said, "This may sound crazy but I love you." Jeri responded, "I love you too." At the end of the evening we hugged again and spiritually, from that moment on, have never let go.

What a perfect fairytale, boy from Brooklyn finds his girl from San Diego; she is beautiful, strong-willed, financially successful. He is creative, some say good-looking, open to growth and warm of heart. I knew that I wanted Jeri in my life and my instincts and intuition knew that complete vulnerability, from day one, was the way to her heart. Taking a very, very big breath, I shared how I had grown in so many areas of my life; however there is this one area that I am very uncomfortable, "I just haven't figured out how to make money." Jeri lovingly responded, "That's great because I do know how to make money." In that moment a great partnership was born.

So here was our situation. Jeri was a successful Real Estate Broker making almost six times more than the $20,000 a year I was making selling copiers. Through Jeri's life experiences and journey in consciousness she realized that she could only count on herself to eat *and be successful. As a result, she had decided that she would give herself everything she hoped a man would give her and set up camp on her dream horse ranch in East San Diego County. Amazingly and thankfully, Jeri was able to look beyond my limited money consciousness; we fell in love and soon thereafter Jeri invited my sons Dan and Tyler, me and our dog, Jenny, to move into her home and a wonderful journey full of challenges and growth took flight. After moving in, it became painfully obvious to me, as a man, that Jeri did not need me for her success. It also became obvious to me that this tough, business-minded woman had a little girl inside dying to get out, if only it was safe. I knew full well that this woman was a key to my happiness in every area and I knew I might learn a thing or two about money-consciousness if I was a willing student. Finally, I knew that regardless of my then-current financial status, that I had a great and honest love to share with her that would richly fill her heart.*

It was 1979 and I was a foot soldier in the copier business. I was given a territory and a gurney type cart and a pat on the behind; well, not literally. Many days consisted of going door-to-door meeting receptionist after receptionist whose job was to screen salespeople, take a card and say the magic words, "We'll give you a call if something comes up." This process was brutal to my spirit, especially because I had been very successful in education and, as a result back then, felt very significant for what I was contributing. While my relationship with Jeri was growing in so many ways, my relationship with my money-consciousness, i.e. myself, was not a happy tone.

Jeri and I had been involved in a series of personal growth seminars and one night on the way home; I shared how frustrated I was with myself in the copier business. My thoughts were that I should find another career because I certainly wasn't enjoying the rejections to my efforts. Jeri wasn't buying, pulled the car into a parking lot, turned the ignition off and asked me if I wanted to handle my money case, right now. My response was a resounding yes."

What Rod is about to share with you, while appearing to be about his life alone, is really about a spiritual process where fundamental internal principles are at work, principles that you can access within yourself. What's so powerful about this example is the speed in which new thought created new form. Pay attention, relate it to you and enjoy the journey.

"So here we were sitting in a parking lot, nowhere to hide and challenging myself to be vulnerable and expose my true thoughts. Little did I know that I was in for a three-hour ride in money-consciousness and when you hear the entire story and especially the results, you will realize the phenomenal and life-changing return on investment for those three hours.

Jeri started by presenting a scenario to me. She knew I loved visualization so she described a scene where I am driving and pull up to a light and a Mercedes convertible pulls up next to me. In the Mercedes is a woman with diamond jewelry on her wrist, neck, ears and fingers. To stimulate me even more, she went on to describe the woman's white Toy Poodle whose collar and leash were sparkling in diamonds as well. Well before Jeri asked me the question, I already was in judgment about the excesses. Jeri then asked me what I thought of the woman. My response was instantaneous, that this woman was materialistic. Jeri pointed out that my face had changed as though in pain and asked me how I

STOP AND TAKE A DEEP, HONEST INVENTORY OF WHAT YOU BELIEVE ABOUT MONEY AND WHAT YOUR PARENTS AND OTHERS AROUND YOU BELIEVED SO THAT YOU CAN HAVE A FIGHTING CHANCE TO MODIFY YOUR OLD BELIEFS AND CREATE NEW THOUGHT THAT IS AUTHENTICALLY YOURS.

was feeling and I indicated that I actually felt disgust. She said, 'great,' and added another scenario. A man pulls up next to me in a Rolls Royce smoking a cigar. The man has a Rolex and gold chains around his neck. Again my reaction is that he is materialistic. Jeri pointed out that in each case, when someone appears to have money that you judge them as being materialistic, you react and obviously do not want to be like them. She nailed it right on the head; then came the magic moment of discovery as Jeri pointed out a principle that was at work here. **Because I disdained**

what looked like money, every time I moved toward having money, the money would move away at the same speed because fundamentally, I did not want to be what it looked like to me. *I DID NOT WANT TO BE MATERIALISTIC.*

My reaction was so automatic and, as such, lacking in conscious reason or thought. It became so obvious that what got poured into me as a child was at work here. Now I was really excited and we dug deeper and I discovered that I had a belief that if you had money you would be inclined to be less loving and since loving is something I prided myself on being, money couldn't be that important. Bottom line was that I realized that my subconscious beliefs would fight like hell to keep the status quo and that I would <u>never</u> have significant money in my life if I continued to allow my inherited limiting beliefs to dominate my thought.

Now my curiosity was on fire and I asked Jeri how to overcome these thoughts that were poured into me. She replied that I had to create new thought to replace them. **One way to start is to bless people who you perceive to have money.** *Think well of them and when you are with someone who has attracted money into their life say, 'good for you.' I tried it on. I thought of someone I knew personally with money, blessed him and noticed a favorable shift in my consciousness seeing him in a different light. Jeri pointed out to me an incredible principle that,* **"until you can bless others for their good fortune, you will not attract it into your life."**

At this point, Rod was excited about his discovery that his resistance to money was simply based on what had been poured into him as a child. With such a gift of discovery, he thought he was done; however I knew that there was significant work that still needed to be done for him to break through so I asked him if he really wanted to dig in and get to work on new thoughts. His response was an enthusiastic "yes" and he began another two-hour journey to his true authentic self.

"Jeri asked me a question that was easy for me to relate to. She asked me: 'How much money do you want to make in a month?' After some reflection I answered $3,000. Jeri asked me why $3,000. I told her that I was making about $1,700 a month in commissions and that my true overhead was about $2,000. If I made $3,000 I would have an excess of $1,000 and more importantly, could take you (Jeri) to a restaurant and not feel the bill. What I didn't tell her, at the time, was that it would also make me feel more like a man, a provider. Jeri pressed on. Jeri asked me if this number, $3,000 was real for me, and could I own it and could I actually feel it. I said yes because I could feel it. Now comes the reality check. Jeri asked me if I was willing to have it happen.

My mind froze and finally it yelped out, 'What?' Then words flew out of me explaining that she didn't understand, I had no deals working and that I couldn't make it happen because we only had two weeks left in this month, blah, blah, blah! Boy did I feel righteous, reasonable and logical with my answer *and I continued until Jeri told me to stop. She asked me again how much money I wanted each month and again why. She pressed me to explain my reasoning for choosing $3,000 and again for what that $1,000 extra each month would mean to me.*

Again, I imagined taking her to a restaurant and not feeling the bill. This part was real for me. But then she got right back to the nitty gritty of my consciousness. 'Was the $3,000 real for me, could I feel it, could I own it and are you willing to have this happen?' Again I repeated the obvious that I had no deals working and that she didn't understand the realities of the copier world and besides, there were only two weeks left in this month and no way was that enough time to pull it off. Still in the car and the parking lot, Jeri again told me to stop defending the position that I could not do it."

I'd like to take a diversion here for a moment. Years ago, an author by the name of Richard Bach wrote a wonderful story about individual freedom called *Jonathan Livingston Seagull*. Neal Diamond, the singer, made it into a song and a movie was created based on the book. Richard's next book was called *Illusions: A Handbook for a Reluctant Messiah*, basically you and I being the reluctant messiah in our life. Throughout the book there are powerful and poignant sayings that strike a chord in our consciousness. Given what Rod just shared with you about his reasoning for not being able to create $3,000 that month, it might help to hear Richard speaking to each of us. **"Argue for your limitations and sure enough they are yours."**

"Jeri shared with me other concepts about how we attract to our life where we are coming from in consciousness and that we repel away that which we are not in harmony with. In essence, that every time I moved toward money, it moved away from me at the same speed because fundamentally I did not want what it looked like to have money. I thought I had hit the jackpot with this understanding until Jeri took me back to reality with the current process about <u>what I wanted</u>, <u>why</u> and was I <u>willing</u> for it to happen. Finally the breakthrough happened. After about two hours, the limiting argument inside of me suddenly went quiet and I answered a resounding 'yes' to my willingness to have it happen. Jeri turned the ignition on and we drove home in silence. I noticed that my mind was absolutely at peace and that there was no self-talk going on. I slept like a baby.

Jeri always shared this quote with me: 'If you are praying for potatoes, reach for a hoe.' The next morning I reached for that hoe and went to work. Something was very different for me. I noticed how everyone and everything seemed more alive and I was excited to be in the office. I had just sat down at my desk when a note was passed to me that, at 9:07AM, Grossmont Bank had called and asked me to call them today. I called immediately and they told me that they remembered me, that I had been in six months earlier and that they were ready to replace some copiers. I went out there to replace their copiers and earned about $2,000 in commission. Later that day, I went back to the office *to do the paperwork and another call came in. This one was what we in sales call a 'blue bird' because it was totally unexpected and out of the blue. I went out, demonstrated a copier and walked away with a sale worth about $700 in commission.*

At the end of the day I was driving home thinking, with excitement, how I can't wait to tell Jeri that I had made $2,700 in just one day. Then this voice deep inside of me said: 'Wouldn't it have been great if I had made $3,000 that day.' It was an old familiar voice with the obvious inflection that not only did I not make it happen (failure) but, more powerfully, that it couldn't happen. Good old inherited limited thinking. I decided to make a stand and told the voice to shut up. I looked around and saw a building, parked the car and walked up to an architects' office. I saw a woman with a purse over her shoulder at the door locking up. I explained to her that I was in the copier business and that it was 4:55PM on a Friday night and that it was the worst time to call on her. She looked at me incredulously and said, 'I can't believe you walked in here tonight; this copier broke down for the third time and my boss said to replace it.' She then asked me if I could come back on Monday. I said I could and added that I had a copier in my car that might fit their needs and that if she was willing; it would take me about five minutes to

IF YOU WANT SOMETHING GREATER IN YOUR FUTURE, CHECK IN WITH YOURSELF ABOUT YOUR WILLINGNESS TO CREATE YOUR RESULTS BY CHOOSING YOUR THOUGHTS.

set up for her to see it. She agreed and lo and behold bought the copier right off my cart.

As I got in my car, I sat and pondered what had just happened over the past 24 hours. I saw, with measurable results, what happened when I was <u>willing</u> to have results in my life. I then took out the paperwork and calculated that this sale gave me a commission of $400, which meant I made $3,100 that day. Calm came over me as I realized what I had just witnessed; within my own being was a spiritual process at work. I felt humble and grateful that I was blessed with this gift to partner with the Infinite Intelligence. When I got home and wrapped my arms around Jeri, I shared quietly about my newfound money-consciousness. It was a very special moment that Jeri and I will always remember for it was the beginning of a new era in thought for me. Following that moment, I never again could deny the connection between my thoughts and the results in my life. I put my spiritual sword in the ground and vowed never to forget the truth I now know."

What was so great about what happened in Rod is that his shift in consciousness was so specific and so measurable. Never once did he think it was a fluke and he went on a journey of growth in which he continually would find himself again telling that old voice in his mind to shut up. He also embraced the concept that a thought is not fact. That it is just a thought and it can be changed. Then he learned a new approach. He found he could actually command his mind to send up supporting thoughts in place of the negative, and guess what, it did. He grew from the copier business and found himself trusting that each business enterprise he embraced was perfect because it was what the Universe was putting in front of him in which to grow. He truly understood that he was a co-creator in this process and his results emulated his growth in both vision and consciousness.

> *"The wonderful update to this story about the $3,000-day took place in early 2002 while Jeri and I were in our CPA's office discussing our taxes. Quite frankly, I don't spend much time on the actual amount that I create because it is simply a measurement of my <u>prior</u> consciousness; I focus on what's next. So here we were with our CPA and Jeri pushes a piece of paper and a calculator my way with a dollar amount which was our income in 2001. She asked me to divide that number by 365 days. I was humbled and grateful as I pressed the equal key to see that, for the first time, I had earned $3,000 a day, every day in 2001. I looked at Jeri with a knowing smile and quietly remained in gratitude with myself, my loving partnership with Jeri and for the blessings bestowed upon me through my being open to the Infinite Intelligence that connects everything in existence." -*
>
> –Rod Walz

Take a moment and think about the process that Rod went through and ask yourself about your response to the woman and her Toy poodle with the diamonds and the man in the Rolls Royce. Notice your thoughts. Can you see yourself in the Rolls Royce? Think of someone you know with money. What inner talk do you have about him or her? Check in with yourself to see if you are truly willing to grow and quiet the old voice inside of you. Create new thought and bless those with money as you would want to be blessed if you had it. Have a vision that all the money in the world already exists and is in motion. Who better to have it than you? Know that you are deserving of all the great things that money can provide. It is important to do a gut check to see how you really feel about having money. Whatever you are feeling, are they your true beliefs causing your feelings or is it just a mirror of inherited limiting beliefs? If you truly desire money in your life, you will need to check your feelings often and create new thought patterns. The old thought patterns got you where you are today. New thought will take you to tomorrow and your desire if you create thoughts that allow money and love to flourish.

UNDERSTANDING YOUR BELIEF ABOUT MONEY

In Chapter 1, I introduced the question, "What do you believe about money?" In Rod's case, it is easy to see some of his beliefs about money and people with it. It is now time for you to be introspective and look inside to discover what you believe about money. This is critical for you because the Law of Attraction is always at work and you will attract that which you believe in. See how important this is! What if you discovered that, like Rod, you too were raised to believe that people with a lot of money are cold, greedy and/or materialistic? Fat chance that money will want to come your way as there is no fertile soil for it to land in and flourish. So it is critical to stop and take a deep, honest inventory of what you believe about money and what your parents and others around you believed so that you can have a fighting chance to modify your old beliefs and create new thought that is authentically yours.

In order to help you, I am including some excerpts from a questionnaire Rod and I created and use in workshops to help stimulate your awareness. It focuses on your father's and mother's beliefs about money *prior to you being 12 years old* and also on your current beliefs. On a personal note, Rod and I completed this questionnaire and had a blast discussing what we uncovered. By the way, it would be beneficial, if your parents are alive, to have them complete the answers to the related questions below. Also, if your children are old enough, it would be insightful for you to hear their answers. Note, if you were raised in a single parent home or even without parents, adapt the questions to those who were present in your life before you were 12 years old. Also, if you don't remember what your parents said about money, just write down what you think they felt or thought about money. Instruction: Write the first thing that comes to your mind. Have fun and here we go:

1. What is your first memory of money?
2. Complete this sentence: "Rich people are
   ....?"
3. "Money is
   ....?"

4. How much cash in your pocket or purse would make you feel uncomfortable and why?

5. What is the most amount of money you made in a year?

6. Who controlled the money in your household? Who was the breadwinner?

7. Did your mom and dad argue over money and if so, what about?

8. What did your dad do for a living? Salaried or commissioned (if applicable)?

9. What do you remember your dad's income was each year?

10. What did your dad say about money?

11. What did your dad say about people with money?

12. How much cash did your dad carry?

13. When you asked your dad for money, how did he respond and how did you feel?

14. What did your mom do for a living? Salaried or commissioned (if applicable)?

15. What do you remember your mom's income was each year?

16. What did your mom say about money?

17. What did your mom say about people with money?

18. How much cash did your mom carry?

19. When you asked your mom for money, how did she respond and how did you feel?

20. What is the largest amount of cash you have had in your personal possession?

21. What is a lot of money to you?
22. If you made a lot of money, what would change in your life?

Your answers above are the beginning to your understanding what is in your money-consciousness soil today. Remember, the subconscious mind seeks that which is familiar and what is familiar are the money beliefs in your soil, <u>regardless of what you say</u>. You may have some work to do. By the way, we all do. Everyone is at their level of consciousness based on past beliefs and because the Law of Gestation takes time, it is important to get at choosing more expanded thoughts and dreams immediately if you want something greater in the future. Always, always check in with yourself about your willingness and faith that you have the power to create your results by choosing your thoughts.

A CONVERSATION WITH THE AUTHOR ABOUT MEN AND WOMEN

Tell the truth quickly and keep breathing! And... Everything happens within the relationship.

–Rod and Jeri Walz

You have read through the book and I have spoken a great deal about your internal work; the work you do just on yourself to create the life you desire. Now I want to speak to you about behavior when it comes to the opposite sex. When we are new in relationship and all the chemistry is flowing, everything seems easy. We naturally give each other all the attention the other can possibly desire. We only see the best qualities in the other person and we let them know by our words and our actions that we think they are the best thing ever.

When time goes by, however, we begin to feel comfortable in the relationship and often we forget to give all that we can to our significant other and, little by little, a distance can begin to form. You don't even see it coming but one day you realize that the bloom has faded between you. It makes me sad when I hear people say things like, "We just fell out of love." You see, love is a choice and it is active. To receive love, we must give it. We must show it in words and actions. When we stop doing this, the feeling that we call love fades. True love is eternal. What most people call love is actually lust. When you love someone, you care about them at such a deep level that their happiness becomes the most important thing in your life. When we are busy asking what they can do for us, we are not loving them.

When Rod and I decided over 30 years ago that we were going to create a life together, we made two rules to live by in our relationship that, for us, has been such a help during those times when we have felt a bit at a loss with each other. The first rule is simply, "Tell the truth quickly and keep breathing!" Sometimes we may have things going on inside us that we do not want to share with our partner but if we do not share it, we withhold it; we create a wedge between us. It can be a little wedge but the wedge will grow over time and little by little as you have more withholds, the wedge gets bigger and bigger and then you wonder what happened.

The second rule is also simple; we said that from this day forward, "Whatever happens in our lives happens within the relationship; including thoughts of leaving." So if we have thoughts of leaving, that is, wondering what life would be like without this other person, then we know that we are in trouble within the relationship. It is important not to withhold these thoughts because they will not get better on their own. It is important to have agreements with each other that you can speak up and say that you are in trouble and find yourself thinking about what life might look like single. Tell the truth quickly and keep breathing, knowing that the thoughts you have and share are all happening within the relationship. In other words, no one is leaving.

Open up a safe space to share all your thoughts responsibly. It is rarely about the other person, it just looks like it is. When you share responsibly, you are not blaming the other person for how you feel, you recognize that the feelings you have are yours and they stem back to your old "stuff" that has nothing to do with this person you love and who loves you. Commit your life to each other and to the relationship. Protect it fiercely.

So right now I want to speak very specifically about how to behave with each other. What do we really need from each other? What do we want but do not know how to ask?

Ladies and gentlemen, it is important to understand the basics about each other in order to make your relationships work. Before I go into this I want to place my disclaimer in here. If there is addiction or abuse in your relationship, you need to seek professional help and what I am about to say may only apply in part. Otherwise what I am about to reveal to you applies to all men and women that I have ever spoken with about relationships.

I will start by addressing the ladies. Ladies, I know what you want in a man because I want the same thing and believe it or not, you most likely have it now only you do not recognize it or your behavior has caused your man to behave in a way that is not in alignment with his true nature. I know this is a big statement and I do not know the man in your life nor do I know you, but just bear with me as I go through some basic truths about men.

Despite what you and your girlfriends have been saying about men up to this point, the truth is that what he wants more than anything is to produce for you. He just really wants to make you happy. He is trying so hard to make you happy that he may have gotten lost in the process and you may have lost interest in him. It is important that you understand this basic fact about men; they want to produce for their women. We make it so difficult for them sometimes. He is hardwired to produce for you. Think about that for just a minute. What if it was true and you knew it to be true; would you look at him differently? If you knew that all you had to do is learn how to ask for what you want in a way that he could understand, would you be interested in learning more?

You see the biggest problem is, as I see it, we women have been giving mixed messages to men for decades. I am not saying it is your fault. We have been living in confusing times with all the demands that are on us in these modern times. Along the way, most of us have been hurt in a relationship with a man so now we tell our men that we like "nice" men. We want them to be "nice". Now, given the fact that they are hardwired in their DNA to want to produce for us, they go about life doing all they can to make us happy by being "nice". What happens then is most confusing to us and particularly to them; we then lose interest in them. They are just too "nice". What happened? Everyone wants to know!! Suddenly the first "bad boy" that enters your life, and he will, looks very attractive to you and your "nice" guy just can't compete.

What happened is that we have misspoken our true desire. What we thought we wanted really wasn't the case. What we really want is, ladies, see if you agree: we want our man to be strong, confident, decisive, and kind. We want him to take care of us, even though we make it very difficult for you men to do this. Women want their man to take care of her heart. Women want their man to protect and care for them. It is true. Even though we women do all that we can to show you how independent we are and capable and competent; we still want you to see and care for the little girl in us. Gentlemen, do not degrade women in anyway. Give your woman the respect she deserves as the amazing, competent woman that she is but know that she wants you to take care of her heart more than anything.

Ladies, you need to let your man know how much you appreciate him and every little thing he does. Know that what he does, he hopes it will produce happiness for you. Even if his only household chore is to take out the trash, when he does it, thank him for it and let him know how happy that makes you. He will notice that you appreciated his efforts and it will motivate him to do more. If he feels successful with you he will continue working in that direction. It is important to let him know that everything he does you notice and appreciate. Appreciate that he works hard for the family. If he opens the door for you, let him know that it means something to you. Ladies, never deny him the opportunity to do for you. And always, always let him come away with a win through your verbal and physical touch appreciation.

How many times has he offered to do something for you and you say, "That's okay, I can do it"? That really isn't the point. Let him do for you. How often have you jumped ahead of him to do something and not even given him the chance to do it for you? If you do this often, then he can't win and will retreat from even trying to help.

The truth is we women can do anything a man can do and we can have babies too, but that is not what makes us feel fulfilled. Women don't want to always be the producer; men do. Yes, men and women all need to feel productive but they are driven differently. So you may be wondering, "If all he wants to do is make me happy, then why doesn't he do more for me?" That may be a complicated question. First of all, he may not have a clue what you want. Do you? Have you let him know what you want in a way that makes it possible for him to produce for you?

Firstly, you have to make him know that he is your man; he is the king in your life. Then you need to let him know how he can produce for you. An example might be Valentine's Day, or your anniversary might be coming up and he may not remember, and for sure he hasn't a clue what to do for you. Make a list of all things that he can choose from that would make you happy. Be creative here. Make the list as extensive as possible and let him know that anything on that list would make you happy. Give him time so he can look through it and see what he would like to do. He will amaze you. Don't expect him to know what you want. That is a setup for disappointment. If you are like me, you might be surprised to discover that you do not know what you want either. If you don't know, how is he supposed to know?

So make a list:
Dinner out (name 2 or 3 places)
Candy (what kind)
Flowers (What kind)
Picnic (Where, when, with or without wine, etc)
Clothing (Be very specific – especially size)

Let him pick from the list knowing that he is safe, that anything he picks will make you happy. He will be relieved and he will amaze you. Just watch him produce. Be sure and let him know how much you appreciate what he did and that it makes you very happy.

Now gentlemen, step up and pay attention to what she is saying to you. Be strong, decisive and kind. We really didn't mean it when we said "nice", so sorry. I know this has been confusing for you. If it makes you feel any better, it has been confusing for us as well. So it is important that you step up in this relationship in a way that you never have before. You may likely bump up against some resistance at first, because you have set up the rules a different way, but stay with her. Know that she wants you to take care of her heart and she wants you to step up and be the man in the relationship. The thing is, if the man doesn't step up, the woman will. So if you have set up the relationship so that she is the one who is responsible for everything in the household including you, it will likely take some work to move it around to a relationship that is fulfilling to each of you. Whatever you do, do not whine. No whining men. That is not allowed. Speak your truth with strength and conviction and make sure you are being kind to her heart at the same time.

The truth is, we need to take care of each other's hearts. Ladies, we need to take care of our man's heart too. It just may look a little different in the way we do it. Praise your man. And men, let your woman know how beautiful she is to you. We can never hear that too much. When I get ready to go out with my husband and I walk into the room where he is waiting for me to emerge, when he looks up, if he doesn't say, "wow," I turn around and go back to change my clothes. And if I don't touch him often and thank him for the things he does, he starts to become distant. It is important to keep the aliveness in your relationship, no matter how many years you have been together. Rod and I have been together over 30 years and it is just getting better every year. I actually do mean that. In every way we are closer, more in love and more excited about each other than we ever were in the early years.

So let's recap the salient points to remember in relationship:

1. Tell the truth quickly and keep breathing.
2. Everything happens within the relationship including thoughts of leaving (make it safe to share them with each other).
3. Let your man know he is your man and that you appreciate his strengths.
4. If you keep taking charge, he will retreat because he will not feel he can win.
5. Plain and simple, men want to produce for their women, especially when he senses he can win.

6. Get very clear about what would make you happy; make a list and communicate it clearly with your man. (Let him know anything on the list will make you happy.)
7. Men, step up, be decisive yet kind and no whining.

And so, I wish the joy that Rod and I have for every couple and every individual who seeks a partner. I hope this helps as you enter into a relationship or recreate the one you are in now.

With Love,

EPILOGUE

Life has no limitations,
except the ones you make.

−Les Brown

Well, I trust that it has become convincingly apparent that if you want to change the pattern of your results, you must change your thinking and beliefs, no ifs, ands and especially no buts. If you interpret what I am saying as encouraging you to turn away from your current relationship or current faith, etc., that is not what I am saying. I am challenging you to choose to explore your current beliefs so that they become clearly yours and not what was handed down to you. You are worthy to modify and let go of beliefs that don't serve you today, especially those limited beliefs talking through your inner voice. These are typically the beliefs that let you know you are not worthy, not capable, not smart enough, or just plain not enough.

These beliefs, as powerful and embedded as they are, can be re-educated and modified. Sometimes it takes assertive action. Sometimes you have to just tell that inner voice to shut up. You have to choose to change your thoughts and only allow in the thoughts that support you moving forward. Know that the thoughts you are having are only thoughts and you can change them right here and now with a decision to do so. So how do you know when you are up against a limited belief inside yourself? The answer is amazingly simple. When you are in reaction (fear, anger, judgment, etc.) to a situation or person, you react because it hits upon a deeply embedded belief that was caused by a memory early on in your life. In other words, it resonates with an earlier embedded feeling. We only resonate with that which is within us now. When you meet someone who you don't like, it is because you resonate with those qualities within yourself that you don't like. By the same token, when you meet someone who you think is the most beautiful, loving person you have ever met, you would not recognize those qualities if you did not also have them within you. In addition you are constantly putting a vibrational context to what everyone is doing and saying. So when you are in reaction it is because you have decided the meaning behind what you are hearing and seeing. You may or may not be correct but it really doesn't matter. No matter what others say or do it is really none of your business any way, even if the thoughts or words are about you. Your only business is what you think and believe about you. I'm not saying this is easy; however; if you want to grow, consider changing the global context of your life's purpose and reduce it to practice as events and people unfold before you. Here's the real fun part.

The next time you are in reaction to someone or something, stop and be honest with yourself that this is not the first time you have felt this way. So stop making the person in front of you responsible for how you feel. Instead, take this as an opportunity to go to a quiet space and meditate, pray, etc. to go back into your memories for the earliest time, as a child, you felt the same way. When you find that memory, really use your imagination and place yourself in that moment again. Speak with the people in your memory and educate them on what you have learned and experienced in your life by having this moment. For those of you who may have a painful (bad) memory, take an inventory of your life about the people and experiences that have shown up in your life to counter-balance the experience. Life always balances when we take a look at what blessings came from an early experience. Be sure to thank them and especially take the opportunity to come from your power and forgive those who impressed this early memory on you by their actions and words. It is here that you now begin to truly _own your life._

INNER WEALTH AND LOVE

Surprisingly, some people are _afraid_ of wealth and love because they do not want to be greedy or get hurt. This all has to do with paradigms, those early embedded beliefs. Some of us were conditioned to think that wealth is equal to greed and to give yourself freely to another means you're going to get hurt. Just look around you at the natural world. Nature is so abundant and always successful. There is not just one type of tree or flower. It is not enough to just "get by". Nature is fantastically abundant; it's overflowing with colors, variation, scents and an amazing eye for details. Our lives can be this way too.

Why should our human lives be fraught with lack and limitations? Are we not part of nature? To think that humans should exist in a state that is contrary to nature may indeed appear normal in consensus, because normal is what so many are doing, but it is not natural. The fact is that all the money that exists in the world is already abundant, present and flowing. It flows to fertile, creative and courageous soil. If, for example, your inner voice believes you are not skilled enough, not educated enough and not worthy enough then the money has no place to germinate because the soil is toxic. The same holds true for a loving relationship. *If you had this inner toxicity and were unwilling to choose to grow, then who would want to be with you, other than someone who resonates with your toxic inner voice?* I cannot tell you enough how critical this point is to your growth.

You have been given the capacity to grow by the Infinite. All those limiting beliefs are nothing more than opportunities for growth. In essence, they are nothing more than a thought. They are not fact. You can change your thoughts and actually you can recreate your past life by changing the context for it. If you knew and "got" that as a child you were a sponge absorbing whatever someone else put into you, without a filter or without your vote, you might be more forgiving of yourself. As I mentioned above, owning your life is a choice and you have the power to speak back into your early memories and change the context. I promise you that if you spend quality meditative time doing this, you will experience a revived life with a promising future. The Universe is ready to respond to your willingness to grow. Trust what it presents to you and go with its flow.

Thank you for spending your valuable time with me and always know that you are in spirit perfect, whole and complete and connected to the Infinite Abundance that is ready and willing to provide for you at the level of your willingness to grow. May all of life's blessings come through you.

With love,

Made in the USA
Las Vegas, NV
21 February 2023

67927083R00132